Anto..
Theophilus
Boisen:

Anton Theophilus Boisen:

His Life, Work, Impact, and Theological Legacy

Robert David Leas

Journal of Pastoral Care Publications, Inc

Anton Theophilus Boisen:
His Life, Work, Impact, and Theological Legacy
All Rights Reserved.
Copyright © 2009 Robert David Leas
v3.0

Cover Photo © 2009 JupiterImages Corporation. All rights reserved - used with permission.

Journal of Pastoral Care Publications, Inc

ISBN: 978-0-929670-04-1

Library of Congress Control Number: 2009924062

PRINTED IN THE UNITED STATES OF AMERICA

In Memory of
Kent Andrew Leas
1962-1980

Love is forever

ANTON THEOPHILUS BOISEN:

His Life, Work, Impact, and Theological Legacy

Courtesy Wylie House Museum, Indiana University

Anton Theophilus Boisen

Anton Theophilus Boisen: born October 29, 1876; died October 2, 1965; Bachelor of Arts from Indiana University, 1897; Master in Forestry, Yale University, 1905; Bachelor of Divinity, Union Theological Seminary, NY, 1911; Master of Arts from Harvard University, 1923; Doctor of Divinity,

(Honorary), Washburn College, 1938; Doctor of Letters (Honorary Chicago Theological Seminary 1957), Chaplain and Supervisor, Worcester State Hospital, 1924-1931; Lecturer and Research Associate at Chicago Theological Seminary, 1926-1942; Instructor at Boston University School of Theology, 1925 to 1930; Chaplain and Supervisor, Elgin State Hospital, 1932 to 1954, Earl Lecturer, Pacific School of Religion, Berkeley, CA, 1942-43.

By Robert David Leas

Contents

FOREWORD

Even the most ardent followers of Anton Boisen will learn something new in the pages of this book   Robert Leas' painstaking research into Boisen's complex, often turbulent personal and professional life is evident throughout. Followers of Anton Boisen know about his life, but I dare say few of us know it to the level of detail compiled by Robert Leas. Leas has researched Boisen's family background, early origins, struggle for the affections of Alice Batchelder, the details of his hospitalizations, his strong commitment to theology and research as a basis for clinical training, and his sometimes thorny professional relationships with colleagues such as Dr. Philip Guiles, Reverend Russell Dicks, and Dr. Richard Cabot, as well as others. Anton Boisen taught us the meaning of the "wounded healer" well before Fr. Henri Nouwen termed the now popular phrase. Leas has shown us how Anton Boisen lived out his woundedness while sowing the seeds of a movement that would rock theological education to its core. This complete biography captures the essence of Boisen through exploration of his many contradictions.

Anton Boisen lived out many contradictions in his turbulent, if brilliant life. He struggled painfully and, for the most part unsuccessfully, to connect with people. Yet he founded a movement that focused heavily on developing intimate pastoral relationships. He was clearly very stubborn, set in his ways, isolated, and dogmatic.

Yet he had the courage and, as Dr. Robert Preston described, the "singleness of commitment , putting his whole self on the line for his struggles, his use of his own suffering as a servant model for other sufferers and his students, made him a living symbol." Boisen focused on analyzing and researching the state of pastoral and collegial relationships. He advocated struggling mightily with one's painful inner demons and worked with his students toward this end. He trusted his internal process enough to live in the hope of finding spiritual and emotional peace.

Leas accurately captures the drama and poignancy of "Pappy". Boisen passionately believed a connection existed between religious thought and mental illness. He believed that his psychotic episodes were healing for him, a conviction that would be contradictory, even disconcerting for most of us.

Leas's masterful and thorough research into the life of Anton Theophilus Boisen explores even further contradictions in this wounded clergyman. Despite his own inner turmoil, Boisen founded a movement that brought incredible healing and depth to the ministries of many pastors and chaplains and the laity, including myself. He presented the value of studying "the living human document" at a time in history when academic study was supreme. Boisen was an academic who dedicated himself to researching and exploring the inner life. He was convinced such study showed how one could use that inner life to cure souls.

Although it was 40 years ago, I remember how I first caught the vision that I might use my own struggles in caring for others. In the midst of my first unit of Clinical Pastoral Education, I saw the possibility of finding meaning through using that awareness of my feelings in my ministry. It was a transformative experience and changed the direction of my life and ministry. The movement Boisen birthed dramatically changed the lives of so many of his followers, and followers of his followers. Ironically, he could not change his own life.

The CPE movement is known, sometimes infamously, for its use of the verbatim. This Boisen did not support. He had an ongoing conflict with Reverend Russell Dicks and Dr. Richard Cabot, who were convinced of the value of the verbatim. Boisen favored a more narrative theological presentation style. This would lead, in part, to their split in 1930.

Robert Leas portrays Anton Boisen's life with sensitivity and warmth, showing deep respect for the man and his commitment to scholarly accuracy. In Leas' presentation of the personal and professional life of this conflicted clergyman, we see the seeds of our own wrestling, the response of each of us who has gained so much from our commitment to CPE. It has always seemed like a contradiction to me that "Pappy" was committed to research though he stressed the importance of engaging the process of learning through encountering the fears, longings, weaknesses and strengths of the other and of himself. Yet, our beloved "Pappy" never really found the peace he so desperately sought. Nor have we in CPE committed ourselves to his vision for the place of research in the movement.

Leas paints a picture of a lonely man once helped into the hospital by one of his students, who never lost sight of his hopes and dreams for himself or this new movement in theological education. It is a portrait of a man racked by the hopes and desires that he might someday convince the love of his life, Alice Batchelder, to marry him, and to have it all end at her untimely death.

Leas encourages us to more deeply appreciate Boisen's significant place in theological inquiry and practical education for ministry. His students respected and admired him, yet he probably was not very aware of it. I have heard their stories as a third generation follower and they are powerful and moving. My connection was through my supervisor, Clarence Bruninga, who replaced Pappy at Elgin State Hospital. Clarence, who died in 2007, is described in Boisen's book *Out of the Depths* as this "young, bright supervisor" who would be coming to replace him. I can attest to Bruninga's brilliance.

Leas captures the "contradictions" that were Boisen's life and career and the pain those contradictions caused him. He was a man who "studied mental disorders for the light they shed on religious experience," while seeking the religious experience that would lighten the burden of his sometimes strange mental experiences. Boisen believed that his episodes of psychosis were experiences of the divine that he could study. It was through his analysis of these experiences that he recognized the importance of using the "living human document" as an instrument to think theologically. The effect he had on theological education was dramatic and remains so today. Bishops, representatives of judicatories, presbyters, pastors, and students say this action/reflection method of theological education has dramatically impacted their ministries. The process of gaining awareness of self, combined with a spirit of inquiry into the wonders of the divine in others, enables the caregiver to care more deeply for others. That process is as profound today as it was for Boisen.

Robert Leas is commended for his extensive research into the life of Anton Boisen. Leas' commitment to discovering obscure elements of Boisen's history is truly admirable. We are indebted to him for detailing his family history and helping to understand some of the turbulence and struggle experienced throughout Boisen's life. Leas has a remarkable sympathy, born out of his own inner struggles, for Pappy's arduous journey. What comes through in this meticulously researched volume is an appreciation of Boisen's ability to maintain his commitment to his personal and professional path. In the midst of all of his psychoses he always returned to his commitment to ministry and to the church. Boisen always saw himself as a theologian. I would say the same about Robert Leas. He is a researcher par excellence, yet he remains a theologian searching for the place of the divine in his own and others' lives. He has performed an incredible service by opening up the life of Anton Theophilus Boisen to those of us who take pride in our founder's legacy. My hope is that this book will do something similar for those who follow after us.

By
Reverend William J. Baugh, D.Min.
Director of Pastoral Care and Education
Tampa General Hospital, Tampa, FL
Former President of ACPE
December, 2008

PREFACE

In the use of language, I have kept gender identity in the exact quotes from the writings of Boisen and others. I have incorporated an inclusive version with regard to gender, race, and religion in what I have written.

The purpose of this biography is to explore the life, work, impact, and theological legacy of The Reverend Dr. Anton Theophilus Boisen. This will include a biographical narrative highlighting the importance of his method and theological tradition. Presenting Boisen's life, I invite the reader to enter imaginatively into another time and another place and into the experiences of individuals different from ourselves. I have tried to tell the story of Anton Boisen, his family, his religious formation, his colleagues, and his contribution to the pastoral care and education movement with relatively few interpretive intrusions.[1] I hope I have done this in a fashion that is, as much as possible, objective, fair-minded, and true.

Boisen's intent was for seminary students to deepen their understanding of theology by expanding their insights into the nature of the human condition and the religious response through the study of "living human documents." When Boisen wrote about the "living human document" in the 1920s, he meant that the exploration of the depth experiences of people in the struggles that their mental and religious life demanded merited the same respect as do the historic texts from which the foundation of the Christian faith are drawn. Each individual "living human document" had integrity of his or her own that called for understanding and interpretation with his or her religious heritage.

As we get to know Boisen personally through his life struggles and accomplishments, through his writings, his essays, and the oral history and comments of his students and professional colleagues, I hope a practical usefulness of his empirical method of doing theology will enhance theological education today.

Anton Boisen was a research theologian, an empiricist who probed the depths of the human condition as manifested primarily in serious mental disorders. Boisen's research eventually broke open a new understanding of mental illness with the assertion that it was not a taboo subject. He also demonstrated that you can learn theologically from listening to the narratives of hurting people. His theory was that the study of individual life stories can reinforce the fundamental structures of theology while bringing about new understandings of religious experience and the ethical choices between good and evil. This method of learning has contributed profoundly to the development and practice of clinical pastoral education. Professor Glenn Asquith Jr. remarked: "Anton Boisen is the most important historic figure in Clinical Pastoral Education and in Pastoral Theology."[2] With this I am of the same mind.

Because of his own experience with diagnosed catatonic schizophrenia, Boisen discovered that mental illness offered a clear picture into the soul. He set out on a journey of discovery that led him to interpret profound mental disorders as an encounter with God leading either to a new assimilation of character or to a breakdown into further confusion and misery. The processes the patient goes through are simultaneously: (1) the illness itself, in his case, for example, schizophrenia; and (2) the struggle of soul to break through. If the individual comes out of the experience with a higher level of functioning and self-integration, the higher soul (self) has won. If not, the patient has struggled but the effort has failed.

In 1925, Boisen invited three theological students, one to work with him directly and two to work as attendants, plus one student, Helen Flanders Dunbar, to work in social services. These students were to work with individuals in crisis, under his supervision, at Worcester State Hospital giving birth to the clinical pastoral education movement. The clinical pastoral education movement that Boisen started has grown from those four students in 1925 to the approximately 7,000 units of CPE completed in 2007.[3]

Although there has been much scholarship around Anton Boisen found in doctoral dissertations, his own autobiography *Out of the Depths*, issues of *The Journal of Pastoral Care*, the *Chicago Theological Seminary Review*, *Pastoral Psychology*, and *The Journal of Mental Health Chaplains*, there has never been a published biography. This biography of Anton Boisen fills a gap in research and scholarship to date.

A method of research used for this biography was to listen to and transcribe the rich narrative that surrounds Boisen's career. In my research, I have listened to and viewed all of what I could find of existing video and audio tapes and CDs relating to Anton Boisen. I have learned much about Boisen from the oral history material at the Association for Clinical Pastoral Education Office in Decatur, Georgia and at the nearby Pitts Theological Library at Candler School of Theology, Emory University in Atlanta, Georgia. One audio tape is a series of interviews with Anton Boisen in 1952 made by a former student and lifelong friend, The Reverend Francis W. McPeek. This audio material revealed a first-hand experience with Boisen. Further perspectives on Boisen's life were gained by listening to the tapes, videos, and CDs that contain interviews and symposia about Boisen recorded during the past fifty years. Oral tradition and narrative theology by Boisen's former students and professional colleagues was invaluable in recapturing a more direct sense of Boisen as a person. This approach was coupled with a research into his life and work at various libraries, the Hammond Library *Boisen Collection* at Chicago Theological Seminary in Chicago, being the principal depository of his personal files, papers, and photographs.

The pastoral care and theology reflected in the life and work of Anton Boisen are important for those who are Clinical Pastoral Education faculty and students, for those who are seminary faculty and/or students who are studying pastoral care and counseling at the graduate level, and for members of the Association of Professional Chaplains. The American Association of Pastoral Counselors has roots in the beginnings with Boisen's journey. Congregational clergy and interested religious leaders and lay workers in the United States and throughout the world who are committed to the care of the soul can gain from knowing about Boisen's life, work, and theological legacy.

This biography explores how Anton Boisen arrived at a new model for theological education. First coming from his own story, and then from the stories he heard in the mental hospitals where he was a chaplain. My particular interest in Boisen stems from my own identity with his struggle as I had four episodes of Clinical Depression during the 80's and early 90's, one time hospitalized. I am also an Alum of Indiana University and appreciated the opportunity to be on campus at the Herman B Wells Library archives, where I began my research and journey with "Pappy Boisen."

ACKNOWLEDGMENTS

I gratefully acknowledge assistance by the following individuals, libraries, and private collections. Reverend James Gibbons, Emeritus CPE Supervisor, Past President of Association of Clinical Pastoral Education, and a mentor and consultant in my educational journey. Jim read the manuscript in its early stages and gave me suggestions and encouragement. The Reverend Dr. Joan Hemenway, (deceased), Past President of ACPE and Supervisor enjoyed reading through the manuscript. She wrote a letter dated March 24, 2005: "Your work helped me to understand in both new and old ways the psychological complexity and theological creativity of Anton Boisen. You have made a real contribution in clarifying Boisen's theological and religious roots."

John Patton, PhD, Professor Emeritus of Pastoral Theology at Columbia Theological Seminary in Decatur, Georgia read an early version of the manuscript and provided helpful suggestions. Dr. Don Marshall, MD, my psychiatrist, read the manuscript, and he made suggestions from the perspective of a practicing psychiatrist. The Reverend Dr. William McKinney, Ph.D, President, Pacific School of Religion, provided a perspective as an American church historian. .The Reverend Dr. William J. Baugh, D.Min., past ACPE President, currently Director of the Tampa General Hospital Pastoral Care Department, enthusiastically provided input. The

Reverend Dr. James Lawrence, D.Min., Dean of the Swedenborgian House of Studies, Instructor in History of Christianity at the Pacific School of Religion provided a helpful review of the final stages of my manuscript. Malcolm Eugene Stern, Ph.D., former Head of the English Department, Evanston High School, Evanston, Illinois, and long-time close friend, gave valuable insights for the writing of this biography.

The Reverend Glenn Asquith, Jr., PhD, Professor in the Department of Pastoral Theology at the Moravian Theological Seminary, read my work in its final stage of writing, and he provided very helpful suggestions. He wrote: "You have captured the vital heart and soul-story about the man who, in my opinion, is the most important historic figure in CPE and in Pastoral Theology." I appreciate the comments given by The Reverend Allison Stokes, PhD, whose book, *Ministry after Freud,* was a good resource. Grateful acknowledgment is made to The Reverend John R. Thomas, (deceased) past ACPE President and long time History Coordinator who supplied articles and material on Boisen from his own personal collection. Robert C. Powell, MD, PhD, Winnetka, Illinois, a practicing psychiatrist and historian, provided very helpful critique of my manuscript on more than one occasion. Appreciation and thanks to Dr. James H. Madison, Distinguished Professor of History and former chair of the History Department at Indiana University, Bloomington. He read the manuscript and gave constructive comment on relevant style and detail. Thanks is given to Leah Grace Goodwin, recent M.Div. Harvard Divinity School. Her careful research and editing of the Endnotes was a grace-filled use of her talents. Special appreciation to The Reverend Dr. Orlo C. Strunk, Jr. Managing Editor of the Journal of Pastoral Care Publications, Inc. who encouraged my effort at writing at the beginning and provided critique and support over a period of several years.

I am indebted to those who made it possible to do direct research in various libraries: First, to the archivists and staff of Pitts Theological Library of Candler School of Theology at Emory University in Atlanta, Georgia, to Joan Clemens, Aimee Morgan, Kara Homo, and Debra Madera, Archivists. I appreciate the welcome and assistance from Joan Blocker, Assistant Librarian, Soeng Heun Lee, Assistant Librarian, Felicia Reilly, Technical Services Librarian, and The Reverend Dr. Neil Gerdes, Library Director; the staff at the Chicago Theological Seminary Hammond Library. They helped with the files, letters, photographs, and papers of Anton T. Boisen in the *Boisen Collection.* I also reviewed Boisen's library of collected books with the assistance of the Assistant Librarian, Soeng Heun Lee. Thanks to Gabrielle Earnshaw, Archivist, at the Henri J.M. Nouwen Archives and Research Collection, John M. Kelly Library, University of St. Michael's College, Toronto, Ontario, Canada who sent me copies of some of the material on Boisen in the Henri J. M. Nouwen holdings.

A word of appreciation is extended to Francis O'Donnell, Manuscripts and Archives at the Andover-Harvard Theological Library, Harvard University, Cambridge, Massachusetts for her work in research and duplication of correspondence between Anton Boisen and Austin Philip Guiles and the Earhart Foundation (1933-1949), as well as the program for the Earl Lectureship in 1943 in which Boisen participated at the Pacific School of Religion, Berkeley, California. Many thanks to Rev. Katrina Scott, also a recent graduate of Harvard Divinity School, for assistance in supplying material on Boisen's rural surveys from the Andover-Harvard Theological Library, Harvard University, Cambridge, MA. Thanks to Cheryl Oakes, Librarian Archivist at the Forest History Museum, Duke University, Durham, North Carolina, who provided information on the Forest Service days of Boisen. Special thanks to Carla G. Heister, Librarian, Graves Forestry and Environmental Studies Library, Yale University, New Haven, CT who provided Boisen's letters to the Alumni Association at Yale University.

I began my research at the Indiana University Library Archives at Bryan Hall and then at the new Herman B Wells Library. This library contains the Wylie Collection and Dr. William Lowe Bryan's papers some of which pertain to the Boisen story. Valuable photos were made available for the book by the Photographic Curator, Bradley Cook, who spent part of one afternoon talking with Gene Stern and myself about Boisen, his Arbutus map, and other photos. I had personal interviews and communication with Jo Burgess and Bridget Edwards, Archivists at the Wylie House Museum in Bloomington. This museum is cataloguing and preserving memorabilia from the estate of Morton Bradley Jr., Anton's nephew. Valuable photos were also made available for publication by the Wylie House Museum. I was able to look at the files at the First Presbyterian Church for record of Anton's joining the church and record of his mother and his grandfather's membership. This is the first organized church in the city of Bloomington, in 1819. Dr. Glenn Asquith, Jr's, article in the *Journal of Presbyterian History*, Volume 60, No 3, and his 1982 "The Study of Living Human Documents" helped with an overview of the contribution of Boisen to theology

The most important love and thanks goes to my wife, Marjory, who has offered criticism and support and has put up with my months and years of work on this project.

INTRODUCTION

Midway in life's journey, Anton Theophilus Boisen found himself in the dark depths of catatonic schizophrenia; the right path was wholly lost and gone.[4] Abandoned in his own suffering and loneliness, he was surprised by a religious conversion, a transformation that turned his life around. In the midst of breakdown, he found the "courage to be." He used his own suffering as a servant model for other sufferers. He knew the mental hospital environment because he had been a patient himself. Even after recovery he continued to be a patient and suffered conflicts of schizophrenia throughout his life. His suffering provided him with insights to become a source of inspiration for a new way to explore theology.[5]

He stayed with his dream and faced difficult tasks for the well-being of his method of theological education. He set the stage of a new paradigm for doing theology through "living human documents" for out of the simple opportunity of a caring conversation with another came a rich educational method.

In the aftermath of a thirteen-month mental hospitalization (1920 to 1921), he believed that there was a religious dimension related to his fundamental disturbance; and he plunged himself into a life-long exploration of the inner world. He wrote in *Out of the Depths*, "Of the four major psychotic episodes, I believe I can say that, severe though they were, they have for me been problem solving experiences. They have left me not worse, but better."[6] From the outcome of the experience of mental illness came the challenge to theological students and clergy to engage in an empirical approach to thinking theologically. From human experience and the personal feelings of individuals in distress, he extrapolated his own theological point of view. In the early part of the twentieth century, this was ground-breaking for theological education.

"Break down the wall existing between religion and science"

During the nineteenth century, science and religion both underwent dramatic changes. Scientific medicine developed in that century concomitantly with religion being abandoned by some scientists and by a large contingent of the medical community. This abandonment in the medical field was accentuated by the appearance of two New York academicians, John William Draper and Andrew Dickson White, who wrote enormously popular, but highly biased, histories of the relationship between science and religion. John William Draper's *History of the Conflict between Religion and Science* (1875) was a narrative of the conflict of two contending powers, human intellect on one side and resistance arising from traditional faith and human interests on the other. Andrew Dickson White's *The Warfare of Science with Theology in Christendom* (1876) began with these words: "I propose to present an outline of the great, sacred struggle for the liberty of the sciences, a struggle which has lasted for so many centuries, and which yet continues." These books presented the late sixteenth century Roman Catholic attacks on Copernicus and the trial of Galileo to name two of their references. The impression was that the modern religious critics of Darwinism threatened to rekindle the Inquisition. Draper and White, in public addresses, denounced Christianity as a slave religion that sought to strangle heresy by building fires around heretics.[7]

This view of science against religion gained considerable following among secular scholars during the early twentieth century. Early in the twentieth century there was a study of medical education in the United States and Canada, known as "The Flexner Report" (1910); and as a consequence, American medical schools were being restructured along more scientific lines. Religion and care for the human soul were erased from medical attention. When religion was mentioned, it was typically as a problem and not as an asset to health care. There were a great number of books, articles, lectures, a virtual outpouring, discussing the conflict between science and religion, focusing on Darwinism. Then, there was that hot court house yard in Dayton, Tennessee in the summer of 1925---The Scopes Trial, America's riveting and timeless debate over science and religion.

A similar attitude had emerged on the side of the religious community in the early essays in *The Fundamentals*, a series of popular booklets published between 1905 and 1915 that helped define the religious belief of the Fundamentalists. Princeton Seminary scion of Orthodox Presbyterianism, Benjamin Breckenridge Warfield got into the fray and contributed an article in the first volume of the *Fundamentals*. Therefore, as Boisen came onto the scene, there was a Fundamentalist/Modernist fight going on in Protestantism, particularly in his own denomination, the Presbyterians, around the issue of religion and science that lasted much of his lifetime, and still exists into present time. Creationism vs Evolution is a lively topic in present day United States.

In the midst, Boisen boldly sought to break down the wall existing between religion and science. His work in the medical context related faith to concrete human situations, making use of human experience to come to a more profound awareness of God and God's relationship to humankind. Therefore, Boisen's method of doing theology dealt with concreteness, with events, relationships, and crises in the lives of individuals, and those individuals in society. Our interest will be how his new theological approach impacted him as researcher and educator.

Boisen's theology followed two assumptions:

First, he believed that an empirical exploration of the life story of individuals in crisis would bring about new understandings of the foundation of religious experience and the way for the theological students to think theologically about their encounters with "living human documents."

Second, he theorized that the study of individual cases, listening to the narrative of hurting people, could reinforce the foundational structure of traditional theology, providing convincing implications for the "sin sick soul."

Boisen's theology centered on his research into human relationships, the struggles people have with the problems of sin and salvation at the depths of their being. At the deepest deep, the ambition of the religious life was to become a part of the religious community, the "fellowship of the best." Boisen admitted that this was difficult, but he stayed committed to his goal that students must think theologically about their pastoral encounters and their own identity as clergy. Boisen stated that "the great opportunity for theological students comes not to those who live in cloistered academic seclusion, but to those whose knowledge is being constantly tested and increased through actual service to human beings in need."[8]

A major goal of this current study is to explore the roots of Boisen's theology.

First, his theology respects the early religious tradition of his grandfather, The Reverend Dr. Theophilus Adam Wylie; and his close relationship with Dr. William Lowe Bryan, both members of the faculty at Indiana University. Theirs was a questioning and logically alert view of the Christian faith; with strong emphasis on the reality of God's Providence. To a degree the Covenanter Presbyterian Calvinism of his grandfather's household remained throughout Boisen's life.

Second, his theology represented the more liberal religious experience of his relationship with his mother and membership at First Presbyterian Church in Bloomington, and the memory of his father; and particularly in his adulthood, the influence of the theological liberalism formulated by professors George Albert Coe and William Adams Brown of Union Theological Seminary in New York. All had a strong impact upon Boisen and his progressive theological perspective and model for learning.

Boisen found a "middle way" in his theological development. He was able to meld the traditional Reformed Presbyterian theology of his childhood years in the household of his grandfather with the insight into human life and religious experience that he gained during his theological studies at the liberal Union Seminary in New York City. The Social Gospel of the early years of the 20th century prevailed at Union Seminary during Boisen's years of study.

The image of the "living human document" challenged, and still challenges, those wishing to think theologically about what they encounter in the religious experience of human beings. Boisen designed a *contextual model* that became a new and challenging theological hermeneutic.[9] He broke down disciplinary divisions in the mental hospital, and also as he was on the faculty of Chicago Theological Seminary. It was a faculty ready to break into new ground for theological education in the 1920s. Douglas John Hall, Professor of Christian Theology, Emeritus, retired faculty of McGill University in Montreal, Canada wrote about contextuality: "to insist upon the contextual character of Christian systematic thought is to claim that at every juncture Christian intellectual reflection entails serious dialogue with the existing situation of one's world."[10]

TIME LINE FOR
ANTON BOISEN'S LIFE STORY

Born October Hermann, his father, is Professor of German at IU	1876
Family move to Massachusetts	1880
Lawrenceville School, New Jersey	1883
Death of Hermann Boisen **at thirty seven Lawrenceville, NJ**	**January 27,** **1884**
Move back to Bloomington, Wylie house	1884
Shot in the right eye during play, losing sight Burning of the auxiliary building	1886
Indiana University graduation BA	**June 9, 1897**
Religious conversion experience	**Easter, 1898**
French teacher at Bloomington High Tutor in French and German at IU	1899-1902
Meets Alice Batchelder at YWCA	**1902**
Master degree in Forestry, Yale University	**1905**
Forest Service	1905-1908
Forest Assistant in Washington, DC	1908
Union Seminary Bachelor of Divinity Honors	**1908-1911**
Country Church Home Missions Presbyterian Church Rev. Dr. Warren Wilson, Director	1911-1912
Iowa State College, Ames, Iowa campus ministry for Congregational Church	1912
Congregational Church Wabaunsee, Kansas	1913-1915
Congregational Church North Anson, Maine	1916 to 1917
WW I. Expeditionary Forces YMCA France	1917 to 1919
State Supervisor, North Dakota Rural Survey, Interchurch World Movement This venture failed nationally	1919 to 1920
Elusive Alice Batchelder: "My love," **Refuses to marry many times**	**1902-1935**

Mental hospital admission Westboro State Hospital	**1920-1921**
Harvard University MA degree	**1923**
Worcester State Hospital Chaplain and Supervisor	1924-1931
First CPE unit, Worcester State Hospital	**1925**
Chicago Theological Seminary Research Associate and Lecturer	1925-1942
Friend with Dr; Richard Cabot, MD	1923-1930
Hospitalization at time of mother's death	**1930**
Cabot and Boisen part ways after Boisen's second hospitalization	1930
Boisen and Austin Philip Guiles have rift Guiles moves to Andover-Newton Seminary to eventually form Institute for Pastoral Care	1931-32
Move to Elgin State Hospital	**1932**
Dr Helen Dunbar MD moves Council to New York, befriends Boisen	1930
Forms Chicago Council for Clinical Training	**1932**
Develops lasting relationship with Dr Dunbar	1932
Hospitalization at death of Alice at Sheppard and Enoch Pratt Hospital Baltimore, Maryland	**1935**
Active speaking, writing, consulting, five books, numerous journal articles	1935-1954
As Supervisor at Elgin State Hospital mainly resides on hospital grounds	1932-1954
Earl Lecturer, Pacific School of Religion Berkeley, California	1943
Doctor of Letters with honors Chicago Theological Seminary	June 6, 1957
Death at 88 years of age, ashes placed on hospital grounds and at Chicago Theological Seminary	**October 2, 1965**
Service of Commitment Hilltop Cemetery at the Elgin State Hospital	October 6, 1965
Memorial Service at ACPE Convention, Miami, Florida.	October 25, 1965

1

A PLACE FOR GOD, SCIENCE, AND THE CARE OF SOULS

The Reverend Anton Theophilus Boisen brought theological students, under his supervision, into Worcester State Hospital in Massachusetts to learn ministry through "living human documents." He presented a ground-breaking approach to theological education through disciplined learning as the seminary student was engaged in the study of actual life experience. The year was 1925, and he called it "learning pastoral ministry by reading living human documents." The student focused most all of her/his education on books and classroom lecture. Boisen affirmed the need for formal theological study in the classroom and library, but he also believed that theological learning could be achieved through disciplined reflection on pastoral encounters with individuals and groups in need.

Consider the following characteristics of Boisen's personal and professional life.

1. One defining characteristic of Anton Boisen's *personal life* is that he struggled with mental illness. He had three major

psychotic episodes and a couple of lesser incidents. He was hospitalized for schizophrenia, catatonic type, in 1920 and 1921at Westboro State Hospital, Westboro, Massachusetts, in 1930, at Worcester Hospital, Worcester, Massachusetts, in 1935 at Shepherd and Enoch Pratt Hospital in Baltimore, Maryland and one psychotic episode just before his death.. When he went into the nether world of his psychoses, it was a world of "madness." At one time, he believed he was John the Baptist and that his psychiatrist was the Devil personified. During his hospitalization in 1935, his psychiatrist, Dr. Weininger wrote that "he believed that he was injuring me and that the world was going to come to an end, and that I would have to sacrifice my life for his." He talked about changes in the moon. He thought the world could be saved if twins were born in every birth because Christ lost his life every time someone was born. He was restless and had difficulty sleeping. He'd get up and the attendant would put him back to bed. This went on several times each night. When he did sleep, he had dreams about Dr. Flanders Dunbar, Dr. Richard Cabot, Alice Batchelder, Mary Magdalene, and the Family of Four. This Family of Four consisted in the weak accepting from the strong and the imperfect accepting from the perfect.[11] He saw strange meanings in the things about him, and he was sure of only one thing, that things are not what they seem.

Within a few weeks, however, his condition improved. When he moved out of the depths, he was on an innovative plateau where he became a creative, inventive, imaginative, risk-taking researcher and persistent theological educator.

In the midst of this creative interplay of intended resourcefulness and dissonant surprise is found the center of his evocative life story. Personally engaged in a struggle to make sense of his own illness, he functioned professionally as a mental health chaplain, a theological researcher, a seminary professor, and a pioneer in the development of clinical training for seminary students.

He affirmed the belief that in the midst of this most chaotic and confusing illness (Catatonic Schizophrenia) can be discovered a moral opportunity for change, and a caring relationship is the most important facilitator of that change.[12] Again we are reminded what he wrote in *Out of the Depths*, "Of the psychotic episodes, I believe I can say that, severe though they were, they have for me been problem solving experiences. They have left me not worse, but better."[13] Boisen felt that love, *agape* love as defined by the New Testament writers and exemplified in the life, death, and resurrection of Jesus is the defining principle of caring.

2. Another defining characteristic of Boisen's *personal life* was that he was obsessed with a male sexual aberration characterized by fear of "being found out," and the fear of the consequences of sexual drive not controlled physiologically and morally from his point of view. Viewing the human condition as warfare between flesh and spirit, he had a firm opinion that sexual misconduct was incompatible with the religious awareness he wanted.

In the 1935 medical record of his illness when at Shepherd and Enoch Pratt Hospital in Baltimore, Maryland, it is recorded that "at age four he had an episode of physical illness which short circuited his life. He believed this was an episode of masturbation for which his father punished him."[14] The punishment on this occasion was that Boisen was circumcised. This fear of being found out and literally being cut was the cause of much anxiety all of his life. It was not that he felt guilty about his wayward sex interests; but that he feared being "cut, cut off," isolated. That led to feelings of failure. He never did feel the freedom to fail.

3. One defining characteristic of Anton Boisen's *professional life* is that he saw the religious congregation (parish and institution) as the primary laboratory for practical theological education, and people with needs, the main concern. The seminary was the place for religious formation and the supervision of pastoral methods. The attention in clinical learning was on the present, not the distant past; on the lives of people and groups; and not entirely on books. Boisen had a continuous interest in the religious community in which the student, as ordained clergy, would participate. This emphasis on community, and the context of that community, came from the influence of The Reverend Drs. George Albert Coe and William Adams Brown whose liberal theology and Social Gospel had become very much a part of Anton's formation at Union Theological Seminary in New York City. Coe taught, "By exercising social impulses, by forming, criticizing and reforming social purposes, by sharing in the joys and the woes of others, and by sacrifice for the neighbor, we can focalize and intensify our consciousness of social needs. We can intensify it until our real world is preeminently the world of people." [15]

4. Another defining characteristic of Anton's *professional life* was that he considered himself, first and foremost, a theologian engaged in research into the nature of the human condition. As a research theologian he sought to construct a theology with the help of "living human documents," while also pursuing a search for the meaning of religious experience, and especially the relationship between religious experience and mental illness. He had a good background in research: first as a United States Forest Service assistant where he learned research methods under the leadership of Dr. Raphael Zon,

and, second, as one who spent three years doing rural church survey work for the Presbyterian Church. Throughout his career at Worcester State Hospital and Elgin State Hospital, he was engaged in some sort of religious research and inquiry, in particular on the question of the relationship of schizophrenia to religious awakening and conversion. It was reorganization beginning at the very center of an individual's being.[16] He believed that the theological dynamics of sin, salvation, and regeneration were efforts at resolution of the human predicament.

He pursued special studies by means of case records for his research purposes. He used these case research studies in his classes for theological students and parish clergy. In the case studies we discover that his work is intensely autobiographical. Many of his books and articles in religious and psychiatric journals have a strong autobiographical tone Dr. Paul Pruyser from the Menninger Clinic in Topeka, Kansas, and Fr. Henri J. M. Nouwen, who had been a chaplain resident at the Clinic, felt that Boisen was so preoccupied with his own schizophrenia that it overshadowed all of his work. Dr. Pruyser felt that this autobiographical focus on the typology of schizophrenia dominated all of his diagnoses.[17] During his lifetime others questioned his thesis as the symptom of his own personal mental struggles. On the other hand, Karl Menninger, Thomas Szaz, R.D. Laing, Frank Lake, and more recently especially Brian Grant in Indianapolis have supported Boisen's pioneer views.[18] Julian Silverman, one of Esalen's brightest and most prolific leaders and also one of the most visionary and wide-ranging research psychologists of the twentieth century, wrote: "There is mounting evidence that some of the most profound schizophrenic disorganizations are preludes to impressive reorganization and personality growth – not so much breakdown as breakthrough."[19]

Throughout the story of Anton Boisen's life there is a dynamic tension between his life narrative and the rise of a new field of theological education and clinical pastoral care. This tension is a creative interplay of the day-to-day triumph and tragedy in the life of this pioneer theologian and the larger organized context of a community that developed committed to theological learning by means of pragmatic observation and assessment. It has become widely used as an integral part of religious formation. It is as important and relevant for the theological student today as it was in 1925 when Anton Theophilus Boisen began a group at Worcester State Hospital.

2

THE BOISEN FAMILY
THE ENCHANTMENT OF
ARBUTUS HILL

Anton Boisen was a Hoosier, born and reared in Bloomington, Indiana. He grew-up in a highly academic family of university educators in the hills and hollers of southern Indiana. There is something inimitable about this theologian who came from the Crossroads of Mid-America. We find him theologically invested in the traditional religion of his Hoosier boyhood years, while open to the liberal religion of his mature years in New York, Massachusetts, and Illinois. The large extended family and the traditional religious background of young Anton Boisen remained a part of who he was, and also what he moved away from in his adulthood.[20]

Anton Theophilus Boisen was born on October 28, 1876, the first child of Elizabeth Louisa Wylie Boisen and Hermann B. Boisen. At the time of his birth, Bloomington was a town of about 2,000. Dr. James H. Madison, former chair of the History Department at Indiana University, wrote about the "Southern Indiana pioneers who were a people of hogs and hominy, of Bibles and hard work, of family and home. Some of these first Hoosiers, such as their greatest exemplar, young Abe Lincoln, were full of imagination and hunger for learning; most others were content with the old ways of their forebears and reluctant to spend a single penny on taxes, schools, or books. Nearly all prized their individual freedom, their conviction that white men, at least, were all equal and that no man should lord over them."[21]

Bloomington was the site of Indiana Academy, soon to be Indiana University, founded in 1820. In time, the university had a significant impact upon the community. However, for many years of the nineteenth century, Bloomington was an isolated community. It was fifty miles from Indianapolis, and forty miles from Columbus, Indiana. There was no major road leading to Bloomington. In spring, travel was impossible with the muddy clay roads. The railroad ran through Columbus, Indiana, and one had to catch a stage that ran three times a week to come on to Bloomington. However, in 1854, the Monon Railroad was built from Michigan City, Indiana (the northern region near Chicago) to Albany, Indiana, situated along the Ohio River. The railroad went straight through the middle of Bloomington across from the court house. The Monon line brought a growth of industry in Bloomington. It was not long before Anton Boisen was born that the "cutters," who provided many a limestone for buildings in the Capitol of the United States, and Showers Brothers Furniture caused two growing industries to expand and feel its muscles.

Professor Madison reminds us: "At the turn of the twentieth century, Bloomington was still more similar to than different from the nearby towns. The presence of the university made an obvious difference, but that institution's mark on the community was still not large enough to shape it dramatically."[22] Into this milieu was Boisen born. His father came from Germany as a young man; and, as a faculty member of Indiana University, he married one of his university students, Louisa Wylie.

Photo courtesy Hammond Library Boisen Collection, Chicago Theological Seminary (CTS)

Hermann Boisen

How did Anton's father, Hermann Boisen, come to this village and this university at the Crossroads of America? Hermann Boisen was born December 11, 1846, in Flensberg, Schleswig-Holstein, Germany. Hermann's father, Johannes F. O. Boisen, was an organist and music teacher. During the conflict between Schleswig-Holstein and Denmark, Hermann's father favored Germany. His father's mother was Marie Anderson Boisen, also of a German-speaking family in Schleswig. She was the daughter of a Lutheran pastor.[23]

The son, Hermann Boisen, graduated from the Royal Gymnasium in Pölin, Holstein in 1869; and in that same year, he entered the University of Würzburg in Bavaria to pursue a doctoral degree. However, in the spring of 1869, because of family financial losses, he left the university before completing his doctorate. He came to the United States. First he went for a year to St. Paul, Minnesota where Major von Minden, a friend, helped him. He devoted his attention to the study of the school system in the USA. He, then, came to Indiana.

Soon after his arrival in Indiana in 1870, he became an assistant to the President of the State Normal School (Indiana State University) in Terre Haute. For a time, he was Superintendent of Schools in Belleville, Indiana. His enthusiastic work had attracted the attention of some teachers in DePauw University, but when inquiry was made concerning a teacher of modern languages at Indiana University, he was highly recommended. He was offered a temporary position teaching languages in 1870 that he accepted; and in the following year, he was appointed Professor in Modern Languages. He left Indiana University in 1874 to teach a year at Indiana Normal in Terre Haute, but he returned in 1876 and taught advanced courses Hermann Boisen married Louise Wylie in 1873, one of his promising former students.

As Professor in Foreign Languages at Indiana University, he was energetic, compulsive, and driven. Hermann's sense of order and discipline was stronger than his patience and tolerance.[24] Dr. William Lowe Bryan, when he was President of Indiana University, said that "he [Hermann Boisen] was one of the most brilliant men who ever came here." One of the students wrote about Hermann: "He tried to master an entirely new line of thought each year. He was all enthusiasm in lighting our torches...Yet he never appeared discouraged. His brilliancy, his versatility, and his mastery over the subjects he taught and deep philosophic insight made a great contrast between him and me. He would take our papers and grade them every day with great care in order to strengthen our weak places. He neglected nothing in his desire to help us. "[25]

However, in 1880, Hermann Boisen resigned his position at

Indiana University because of the dismissal of a colleague who Hermann felt was unfairly treated. He packed his bags; and he and his family went to Massachusetts where he was appointed as the Chairman of Modern Languages at Williams College in the Berkshires. If he did well, he would have a permanent position. However the position lasted only a year as a new administration did not make the appointment permanent. We find him next in Boston where he taught in private schools. In 1882 he took a position as Sub-master in the Eliot School in Boston, and in the same year was appointed Director of Modern Languages in its summer school on Martha's Vineyard. The position at Eliot School in Boston gave him great pleasure, but it curtailed his writing projects. He had written an excellent *Book of German Prose*, published by D. C. Heath, New York, 1882. In this book, he wishes to introduce the student to the literature of the German language by introducing his reader to the author. He wrote: "It is incumbent open the teacher to remove unnecessary obstacles and to proportion the labor to the learner's need and strength."[26] In 1883 he gladly accepted an invitation to the faculty at the newly formed Lawrenceville School in New Jersey near Princeton University. There he would have leisure to do writing on a projected book.[27]

In remarking on his appointment as Master in Lawrenceville School in 1883, Hermann Boisen wrote, "I shall go there to put my heart, all that is in me, into it. Isn't that the way to do it?" Here seems to be the secret of his unrivaled success as a teacher, for at all times, and in all places, the best and all that he had, even himself, he gave to his chosen work, and with such an earnestness of purpose, such a noble generosity of sympathy, and such a vitalizing warmth and strength, that his influence became an inspiration to his pupils. The head of the German Department at the University of Chicago said that he was one of the most gifted teachers he had ever known.[28] It is said of Hermann Boisen that he gave his life for education.

Herman was a liberal theologically. He belonged to the Congregational Church in Bloomington. Boisen records in *Out of the Depths*. "My father had joined the Congregational Church and on that occasion he wrote out a statement of belief that shows that he was a thoroughgoing liberal."[29] If his father had lived, along with his mother adhering to the more liberal theology, Boisen may not have had such a struggle with both liberals and conservatives.

Hermann's health had not been good. He lived under very high tension, but he went to work with his regular energy and earnestness. He loved the boys under his care. He started a book on *Language Lessons*, a book for use in the public schools. Suddenly he was taken violently ill. However in a couple of days he was up and insisted on going to school.

He taught all of his classes on that Monday, January 27, 1884. At about seven o'clock that evening, he suddenly died of a heart attack. He was only thirty eight. Hermann Boisen was beloved by the boys at Lawrenceville, and they put up a stone on his grave that reads: "Erected by his colleagues and pupils of the Lawrenceville School as a tribute to his worth as a man and his genius as a scholar."[30] Given the type of man he was, it is very unfortunate that Anton did not get to experience his dad as he grew up in this world. Anton was thirteen when his father died.

After the death of her husband, Louisa took Anton and his baby sister, Marie, back to Indiana to live with grandfather and grandmother Theophilus and Rebecca Wylie, in the Wylie family home on Second Street in Bloomington. Anton was born there; and upon return in1884, he lived there until he left Bloomington in 1903.

How did Boisen view his relationship to his father? He wrote in a letter to one of his psychiatrists, Dr. Noble: "The relationship to my father has been, for me, all-important. My father died when I was seven years old, leaving behind his memory which determined my ideals and goals in life. My memories of my father, although coming from my early years, are still vivid; and his influence has been all important in my life. My father has for me become one with my conception of a heavenly Father."[31]

At Hermann Boisen's funeral in Bloomington, the President of Indiana University at that time, Dr. David Star Jordan, paid high tribute to Hermann as a teacher who inspired all with whom he came in contact. Anton cherished this tribute throughout his life. In this tribute, Dr. Jordan described how Professor Hermann Boisen took him out to the arbutus hill. The arbutus flower, "the trail-flower of the Pilgrim Fathers [and Mothers]," became a significant symbol for Anton Boisen in his life.[32] To Boisen the woods and meadows around Bloomington were full of memories of his father; and with the arbutus-covered hill-side, his name should be forever associated.[33] All through his autobiography, *Out of the Depths,* this arbutus flower had symbolic characteristics. He had heard from his mother about arbutus hill that lay to the east of Bloomington and was closely associated with his father's memory. In high school he began to go to arbutus hill and went every spring thereafter as long as he was in Bloomington.[34]

He had discovered a new hill during his second year in college, only to find out that his professor, Dr. William Lowe Bryan, had already found the spot. They promised to keep the fact a secret. Soon after their agreement, Boisen joined Bryan's Bible class at the Walnut Street Presbyterian Church, and read William James' *Principles of Psychology* under Bryan's guidance. This was a foretaste of what was to come. The recollection was to be a blessing and a curse.

Fr. Henri J. M. Nouwen wrote of Anton's father-image: "The

ideal image of the perfect and severe father entered into many of his relationships with his teachers, Alice his muse, and finally with God." Nouwen continues to conjecture that the arbutus is more. "It is related to a major decision in his life: his decision to go into forestry, to answer the call to ministry, and finally with his love for Alice."[35] He joined the School of Forestry at Yale through the influence of the memory of his father. Nature was his father's second choice, however. First was language. Anton prepared to teach German and French at Indiana University. When he did not do so well at teaching after graduation, he turned to his father's second interest, forestry. Boisen wrote in *Out of the Depths*, "This decision to become a forester, like my interest in the arbutus itself, thus grew out of a loyalty to my father's memory that had become one with my religion."[36] Here, again, Boisen identified the idea of God with the image of his father. Throughout his life he was looking for his father and in search of God. The arbutus was the symbol of his search, the Holy Grail of his quest for God.

The arbutus and the memory of his father related also to his call to ministry. He commented: "I had never before dreamed of such a step, but the idea seemed to cry authority from the way it came. It also made sense. It meant that just as out of the devotion to my father's memory, I had been led to discover new haunts of the flower that he loved, so now through that same devotion I had tapped anew the eternal sources of religious faith and renewal."[37]

The final association of the arbutus flower to Boisen was his relationship with Alice Batchelder, the unrequited love of his life. He had taken Alice to the arbutus hill, and there first told her of his love. Alice wanted to end the relationship immediately. He never fully knew Alice, the Grail maiden, as he sought the arbutus, the Holy Grail, symbolizing the conclusion of his quest. Later while in seminary, he had planned an elaborate rendezvous with

Alice in the hills of New Hampshire when its arbutus flowers were blooming, but Alice did not want to go there. She wanted to go to New Hampshire and bring along a friend. He backed out of a proposal to Alice and only took her photographs "twelve exposures…the precious chance was gone."[38] Anton was deeply hurt and brokenhearted. Alice was definitely not the arbutus that was the end of his quest, although he kept hope alive until her death many years later.

The long quest for the arbutus was a search for God, his father, Dr. William Lowe Bryan, and the love of his life, Alice Batchelder. This quaternity of influential individuals, all are connected to his idea of God. Eventually, it is God that shines through the many images to bring holistic meaning to his life.[39]

In a letter to Herman B. Wells, President of IU as 1961 Boisen sought special state protection lands for the arbutus in Monroe County. Herman B. Wells responded in a letter dated January 4, 1961. "The arbutus plant seems to be holding its own pretty well, and I cannot foresee anything likely to happen in the near future which will further endanger it. Apparently much of Monroe County is gong back to its natural condition and the arbutus areas are benefiting. This is comforting." Providence has seemed to protect the arbutus hills for Anton.

At his hospitalization in 1935, Anton had been asked about homosexuality. In a letter appealing for his discharge, he wrote to Dr. Weininger dated the 5th of December, 1935: "In regard to homosexuality, if by that you mean the relationship with my father that has been for me all important. Where this factor of homosexuality enters into this I do not see. Indeed in early life I was oversensitive in the matter of sex, but I never had great attraction or repulsion toward any member of my own sex. My thoughts have been always centered in the other sex. During my disturbed period, I have done several things which might suggest a homosexual tendency – although back of this there was no corresponding interest" [40]

Hermann Boisen's spirit, vigor, and investment lived on in his son. The dedication and investment that Hermann held was passed on to Anton. As was his father, so also his son, for Boisen was an invested, earnest, driven individual as he sought the wisdom to understand and interpret the experience of his mental breakdown in the light of religious experience, to overcome the sense of isolation and alienation and be set free to be a part of the Fellowship of the Best.

THE WYLIE FAMILY
DEEP ROOTS IN HOOSIER
ACADEMIA

Courtesy: Indiana University Archives

Anton is on grandfather's lap and mother and Marie are second on the left of Theophilus This picture was taken in 1880 on the 70th birthday of Professor Theophilus Adam Wylie

Anton Boisen was a Hoosier Pioneer. His maternal family was among the founders of Indiana University. The Reverend Dr. Andrew Wylie, a Presbyterian minister, was a cousin of Boisen's grandfather, Theophilus Wylie. Andrew Wylie was inaugurated as the first President of Indiana College on October 19, 1829. Wylie was the third member of the faculty, joining The Reverend Dr. Baynard R. Hall, Professor of Ancient Languages and The Reverend Dr. John H. Harney, Professor of Mathematics and Natural Philosophy and Chemistry. Dr. Andrew Wylie was Professor of Moral and Mental Philosophy, Political Economy and Polite Literature. All three faculty members were Presbyterian, as were the university presidents until 1865. In the beginning there were 30 students and two faculty members. By 1851, the final year of Andrew Wylie's presidency, there were 163 students.

In his inaugural address, Andrew Wylie emphasized the advantages to Indiana of the liberal education of students in the four professional areas of law, medicine, theology, and pedagogy; but he never really settled into southern Hoosier life in the wilderness that southern Indiana would have typified then. He remained a sophisticated, somewhat aloof, Ivy League graduate and professor. What the university needed was a president who could understand Hoosier idiosyncrasy to lead people to actively support the university. Andrew Wylie was not such a man. He never understood the Hoosier mentality and their differing views

Professor L. C. Rudolph wrote, "Often the families from the east did not fail when they refused to identify with back-country culture. They were a healthy corrective on the frontier because they represented another cultural and religious standard which the frontiersman needed to remember and to face."[41]

Andrew Wylie in 1837 joined the Episcopal Church because of the quarrel between the Old School and New School Presbyterians. Wylie held with the New School. In 1831, the General Assembly of the Presbyterian Church was divided into what came to be called Old School and New School parties. It was over adherence to the

Standards for Ordination in the Presbyterian Church, the direction the American Home Missionary Society, and its rival the Board of Missions of the Presbyterian Church, and the emerging anti-slavery agitation among mainly Presbyterians in the North of the USA. When the Indiana Synod and Vincennes Presbytery went in favor of the Old School, he withdrew and united with the Episcopalians.[42] Wylie opposed the anti-abolitionist Old School Presbyterians[43] regarding slavery. Andrew Wylie was an active abolitionist. He eventually became an ordained Episcopal Rector.

: Hammond Library Boisen Collection, CTS

The Reverend Theophilus Adam Wylie

Margaret and Samuel Wylie had five children. Their first son, Theophilus Adam Wylie, was born October 8th, 1810. This was Anton Boisen's grandfather, a significant figure in his early childhood and youth.

The Reverend Theophilus Adam Wylie was educated in Philadelphia, and he graduated from the University of Pennsylvania in 1830. He was rewarded by receiving Phi Beta Kappa. In 1836, after theological seminary, he was ordained and licensed to preach by the Reformed (Covenanter) Presbyterian Church. Although he did not want to be a minister as he later wrote, "it seems it was my fate. I was thrown into the current. " In 1838, he said: "My preaching is so bad, I would not want to listen to it."[44]

Boisen's grandmother, Rebecca Dennis, was from Germantown, Pennsylvania, was married to Theophilus in 1838. In a letter (March 29, 1837), his cousin Dr. Andrew Wylie, then president of Indiana College, offered Theophilus a faculty appointment as Professor of Natural Philosophy and Chemistry in the nascent state college in Bloomington.

> D[ea]r Cousin, At a meeting of the Board of Trustees of Indiana College held yesterday you were unanimously appointed to the office of Professor of Mixed Mathematics till the next regular meeting of the Board with a salary of $800 per annum. The appointment was thus made pro tem. in pursuance of your own preference as expressed in your letter. Should you on trial of yourself . . . give satisfaction to yourself & others concerned you may expect the salary to be raised to $1000. Should you accept, please lose no time in setting out. I will expect you at the very furthest by the first of May at which time the next college term commences. Andrew Wylie, Bloomington, Indiana to Theophilus A. Wylie, March 29, 1837[45]

Theophilus left Philadelphia immediately. It took him ten days to reach Bloomington, just in time for the new term to start on May 1, 1837.[46] Rebecca Dennis Wylie gives a colorful view of conditions in Bloomington 1838 when she arrived.

> When I came here in 1838, things were in a rather primitive state. There was no railroad then in this part of the country and the National Road was just being built. We came from Pittsburgh to New Albany, Indiana by boat and the rest of the way. She came to Bloomington in a stage coach drawn by four

horses. The roads were very bad, the stumps of recently cut trees sticking up in the middle of the road way.

When the stage arrived in Bloomington, the coachman blew a long and loud blast on his horn causing the horses to jump and they turned over the stagecoach. Rebecca had to scramble out. She eventually settled into the day-to-day routine of this small college town in the hills of southern Indiana that had just acquired the name Indiana University (1838).

Theophilus wrote in his *Diary* on 2 October 1839: "Last evening, my dear wife has borne me a daughter, a beautiful child." This was, Elizabeth Louisa (Louise) Wylie, Anton's mother.

For forty six years Theophilus Adam Wylie remained a professor at Indiana University. For a period of six months, in 1859, he was appointed Acting President of the University while they searched for a new President. Theophilus Wylie was a versatile scholar. He was a very effective teacher, respected by his students. At various times, when there was a need, he taught all the subjects offered in the curriculum. Often that was necessary in those days. In that mid-era of our American frontier, a professor was asked to cover several fields of learning. He was, during most of his service, a Professor of Natural Philosophy and Chemistry. He also served for 38 years as the university librarian.[47] He remained on faculty until the month of June 1886 when he retired and received the title of Emeritus. He was 77 years old at that time. He had received an honorary Doctor of Divinity from Miami University, Princeton University, and Monmouth College, and the honorary Doctor of Letters from the University of Pennsylvania.[48]

Theophilus Adam Wylie was small of stature, weak of voice, diffident in manner; but he was a man of the old time culture, with the highest degree of refinement and learning. He was a scholar, altogether dedicated to Indiana University. He received Phi Beta

Kappa from his days at the University of Pennsylvania. Although a scholar, he was openhearted and a born gentleman. He had a deep affection for books and left his 1200 volume working library to the University. This included volumes in the fields of science, religion and the classics, representing the breadth and depth of knowledge of a nineteenth-century scholar. In 1880, Theophilus Adam Wylie published a book on the history of Indiana University, *Indiana University, its History from 1820 to 1880,* that is an engaging story of the early years at the university. Theophilus has an Introduction followed by a series of chapters written by different contemporary historians, with a long section on faculty, presidents, students, and university life. He tells in detail the story of his cousin Andrew and his journey in 1828 into the wilderness of Indiana from Washington, Pennsylvania to assume the presidency of Indiana Seminary that was to become Indiana College in 1828 and chartered as a university in1838.

Theophilus Adam Wylie, and his wife Rebecca Dennis, had a family of eight children. When Anton, his mother, and his sister came to live at the Wylie house after the death of Hermann Boisen, there were six cousins who lived at 307 Second Street at that time. Anton Boisen grew up in this home. He was born in this house in 1876, and came to live permanently in 1884 until 1903 when he left Bloomington to study at Yale University. In a Christmas card sent to the Reverend Dr. Austin Philip Guiles, Anton Boisen wrote about his memories of the Wylie home. The card reads in his hand script: "Here is a picture I got last spring of the house which means much to me. It is this old home of my grandparents where I was born and where I lived from 1884 to 1903." He then describes the "Wylie homestead in Bloomington Indiana being built in 1835 by Andrew Wylie, first President of Indiana College, bought in 1857 by his cousin Theophilus Adam Wylie. It was later bought in 1916 from the Wylie family by Amos S. Hershey, Professor of International Law. This house has now become the property of Indiana University and will be preserved for its historical associations."[49] The house was a substantial federal design, red brick, large and prominent for the little town of Bloomington in the early 19th century.

Along with his teaching, Theophilus Wylie was active in congregational ministry. He was a pastor in Bloomington's New Side Reformed Presbyterian (Covenanter) Church.[50] The church he served followed the doctrine according to the *Westminster Confession of Faith*. They were progressive in most areas of the uses of the church in social action. The church differed from the strict Old Side Reformed Presbyterians in that the New Side Presbyterians supported the antislavery movement and were active in the Underground Railroad when to do so was an act of civil disobedience.[51] In worship, Theophilus Wylie did hold to the belief that only the Psalms should be used as church music, and that musical instruments should be forbidden. Sabbath-keeping was regarded as imperative. The Presbyterians had great respect for education. Ministers of the Presbyterian churches came to Bloomington because of the presence of the college.

Anton was deeply respectful toward his grandfather. He was exposed to the New Side Reformed (Covenanter) Presbyterian Church by his grandfather Theophilus. It was one of four Presbyterian churches in Bloomington during his boyhood.[52] He described the church in his way: These churches were characterized by great loyalty to family and clan, by their emphasis upon Old Testament morality, and by their requirement of an educated ministry. Their services were long, their sermons doctrinal and dry, and church attendance was compulsory on the part of all members of the family. Family worship was held in the home everyday, often morning and evening. There was among them no appeal to the emotions, and no attempt to win converts. Their growth came through birth and immigration. [53]

The New Side Covenanters also favored the revivalist movement of that time. Followers of Reformed Presbyterianism affirmed that revivalism was "the work of God's grace among us." They supported the Home Mission movement conjointly with the Congregational churches. All three of these religious activities, the abolition movement, revivalism, and the home mission venture, were liberal compared to the Old Side Presbyterians. [54]

The New Side was especially zealous in maintaining their doctrinal standards for members as well as ministers. There was no public office holding or support of a government that was not God fearing. They endeavored to hold fast to the teachings of John Calvin. Boisen, living within this household since he was seven, integrated certain aspects of traditional Calvinism into the warp and woof of his theology. Professor L. C. Rudolph stated that the Calvinism of Anton's youth fit into his interest in psychology.

"Old Side Presbyterians believed that doctrinal orthodoxy was of primary importance in Christian faith, Old Side men and women desired a strict subscription to the *Westminster Confession.* Old Side men sharply criticized contemporary revivalists. They condemned emotional excesses and demanded that true revivals be carried out within the church guided by its confessional stance on God's sovereignty and human inability. The abolitionist Charles G. Finney's *Theology and Lectures on Revivals of Religion* (1835) was thoroughly criticized."

The congregation that Grandfather Wylie served disbanded in 1889. Reverend Wylie advised his congregation to affiliate with the Walnut Street Presbyterian Church in Bloomington.[55] Reverend Theophilus Wylie's family affiliated with the Walnut Street Presbyterian church.

Anton was 8 when his grandfather started going to the Walnut

Street church. The Reverend Wylie died on June 9, 1895. It was the Junior Year of his grandson Anton's study at Indiana University. His wife, Rebecca, lived on in the house on Second Street until her death in 1913 at almost the age of 101.[56]

Photo by author in 2004
This is the Wylie home in Bloomington built in 1835
Anton's boyhood home as it appears today.

In 1859, Theophilus Adam Wylie bought the Wylie home on East Second Street in Bloomington. Theophilus had an entry in his diary for the 24th of October 1859: "Moved from the old and comfortless house of Dr. Maxwell where we have lived since our return from Oxford, Ohio to the house built by Dr. Andrew Wylie. Altogether it consisted of five acres. A number of the members of the congregation assisted with their hands and teams."[57] It was to this house in 1884, that Elizabeth Louisa Wylie Boisen, and her two small children, Anton, age seven, and Marie, age three, moved. Grandmother Rebecca Wylie welcomed the Boisen family into her family circle. However, she found that having two more children was stressful and trying indeed.

To add to the distress, Dr. David Starr Jordan became President of Indiana University in 1885, and he wanted to upgrade the faculty with young specialists. Boisen's grandfather had to go, unable to complete fifty years of service to the university. Boisen's uncle Brown Wylie, his mother's brother, was also relieved of his office in the chemistry department. In one fell swoop, all of the Wylie's were eliminated from the faculty of Indiana University, ending an era that had begun in 1829.

Anton's mother took a job teaching art in the public schools; and an African-American woman, Lizzie Breckenridge, was hired to cook and help take care of the household. She was a very active member of the New Side Presbyterian (Covenanter) Church that was supportive of the antislavery movement. She served the family for fifty years. Anton remembers Lizzie being the one who took him first to a Reformed Presbyterian Covenanter Church. "I remember going there as a very small youngster in the company of the faithful old Negro woman who for fifty years worked in our home and whose membership in that church is a reminder of early enlistment in the anti-slavery cause. I remember what happened when the congregation raised its voice to song. There was for me something terrifying in that singing, and I also raised my voice – but not in song. I was promptly removed. Some of the old tunes still remain my favorites."[58]

The move back to Bloomington from the prep school in Lawrenceville, New Jersey, meant also a new family to which to relate. Theophilus and Rebecca had 8 children, 6 of whom lived with them in Wylie House at that time. How was this shy and retiring seven year boy to fit into that milieu of six cousins at home? Although he had seen his cousins on several occasions, he'd never lived in such a large household. The move into an existing family must have been a most traumatic experience for young Boisen.

His father had been caring and attentive, spending much time with him walking in the woods and identifying trees and plant life, playing at home when he came back from teaching. In many ways, he never fully got over the loss of his father and the trauma of the change in circumstance during his early childhood.

Boisen endured another childhood trauma when he was shot in the eye by a child's air gun. This produced a scar across the cornea, and he lost eyesight in the left eye. From then on, he saw only one-dimensionally and never experienced the fullest depth of multidimensional sight.

There is also the story of his falling off the high back porch of the Wylie house, tumbling head long down the hill to the garden. His mother and sister were alarmed that he might have seriously hurt himself, but he did not.

There stood a large auxiliary building just off the kitchen door when Anton joined the family on Second Street. It had many practical uses for the household. One day, as Anton was burning bag worms with a hot steel poker, he laid the poker on the floor of the barn, and it caught fire and burned to the ground. The family was angry about this neglectful happening as the near-by small barn was a vital part of the day-to- day household activity.

His grandfather, and the household on Second Street, made a great impact on Boisen's life. The discipline of the household that sometimes frightened him as a child stayed with him, and it resulted in a particular type of a shame-based adult; the shame was especially associated with what he felt in his dealing with (or not dealing with) his own sexuality.

In 1893, Boisen joined the Walnut Street Presbyterian Church[59] in Bloomington where his mother belonged and worshipped. His grandfather and the Wylie family worshipped there too after the New Side Covenanter Church, where Theophilus Wylie was pastor, was disbanded.[60] The *Manual* of the Walnut Street Church, Bloomington, states that "the pastor and his wife will be at home regularly on Tuesday evenings." In the current First Presbyterian Church Archives, there is a letter from The Reverend George Luccock, pastor at that time (served from 1891-1894), inviting Anton to one of these evening gatherings for the new members.[61] In joining this congregation, Boisen made a decision to be a part of moderate Presbyterianism represented in the Walnut Street Presbyterian Church (later First Presbyterian).

Boisen reflected later in life that he did not derive much meaning from the long Sunday morning services, the daily Bible readings and prayers in the strict Calvinist household. He became critical of the Presbyterians in Bloomington as he had known them in his early childhood and youth. He felt doctrine and ritual was of secondary importance to clan and loyalty to the Scottish race. That period of his life, however, did have one positive effect upon his basic view of religion. He learned that a faith experience could matter for individuals. The positive religious life model of his grandfather and grandmother, and his own mother, left an imprint upon him that God was a benevolent God, a God of Providence and vision. In time he became a well informed theologian whose roots were in the theology of the Presbyterian tradition.[62]

Courtesy: Wylie House Museum, Indiana University
Courtesy Hammond Library Boisen Collection, CTS

Elizabeth Louisa Wylie Boisen, Anton's Mother

Boisen's mother, Elizabeth Louisa Wylie Boisen, was born 1839 and died in 1930. She was one of the first women to enroll at Indiana University, being one of seven female students in the class of 1871. Indiana University was all male until 1867. After her graduation, she taught art one year at the University of Missouri. She left Missouri at the end of her first year to be married in 1873 to her teacher of German at Indiana University, Professor Hermann Boisen. Anton Theophilus was their first child and a younger daughter, Marie, was born when Anton was three. Marie later graduated from Indiana University in 1900, married Morton C. Bradley and moved to Arlington, Massachusetts.

Theophilus Wylie kept a diary that he began when he was 19 years old. He had just graduated from the University of Pennsylvania. On the 27th of December 1874, he tells of a get-together with Hermann B. Boisen and his daughter, Louisa Wylie Boisen, in the parlor of the Wylie house. "Professor Hermann Boisen and others arranged a beautiful Christmas tree in the German style. A Balm of Gilead, we used to call it, was placed in the middle of the parlor and decorated with bonbons and lights. The Christmas presents were arranged on the tables around the tree. It was delightful when the appointed hour came to see the joy of all the little ones…" On this occasion, Hermann Boisen brought some of the German traditions into the strong Scotch-Irish Wylie family.

Anton's mother was always supportive of him emotionally, religiously, and financially as she was able. His mother was a good musician and singer. Anton said that his interest in music and the development of a hymnal for mental health came from the influence of his mother, and that during this period of his life, her influence was noteworthy. His mother was a liberated woman for that time. However, traditional Calvinism was very much a part of Louisa's early life. In later years, she had moved away from the more rigid Covenanter Presbyterianism and joined the Walnut Street Presbyterian Church.

Her early religious formation is reflected in a letter to her sister in April 19, 1859. She shares some of the events in the family, commenting on the fact that she does not excel in writing. "I can hardly expect to make my letters very interesting to you as I am at all times a stiff composer." In the letter she mentions the death of a child and the parent's grief. "I believe it was a necessary death that he should be taken to teach him his duty that she believed that he would have gone back into the old path of sin and wickedness. Now, I think he was truly changed." She says, "God sent a special message to him, God did it in love God has spoken several times in prayer meetings."[63] Then later in this same letter she wrote, "God has been merciful, and I do wrong to have such fears. It is because I am so wicked and rebellious that I have such fears. I do not grow in grace, and sometimes I fear I am growing backwards instead of forward, or my heart feels cold when it ought to be burning with love to God. But, I do believe that I desire to love him and serve him with all my fervor. So, if the desire is from the heart, as I know it is, God knows it, and God will not turn away. I have felt some deeper peace lately, but still I do not feel that my whole heart is devoted to my Master's service."[64]

In another letter to her cousin, Jane Harris, she begins with a question: "Are you losing all interest in serious things? I do sincerely hope not for if you grieve and turn away, the Holy Spirit, I fear, he will never again plead with you and you will be a dreadful looser...read the Bible carefully, and with prayer. Have you compared our holy religion with the inspirations and fancies of the world? Is there a better way to Heaven than by Jesus? You cannot find anything so fully, utterly, answering the demands of our nature than which God teaches us in the Bible. If you are in earnest, you will pray to God." [65]

In these letters we get a glimpse of Louisa's early religious point of view. The admonition was to read the Bible. The Covenanter Presbyterians took the Bible literally, and Louisa followed, sharing with her cousin the importance of the Bible. Biblical exegesis and interpretation was central in the sermons of her father.

The strict Calvinist religion is apparent in this letter written when she was 17 at the Glendale Seminary. This firm and serious faith was felt deeply by Elizabeth at this period of her youth. In adulthood, she left this Presbyterianism for a more moderate point of view within the Reformed and Presbyterian religious tradition. Boisen's mother was gentle, retiring and a professionally competent woman. He came to respect her perspective on life. Later, having had this foundation in his relationship to his mother, he showed an interest in the moderate liberal theology that prevailed at Union Seminary in New York.

Anton and Marie Boisen   Marie Louise Boisen Bradley
Courtesy: Hammond Library Boisen Collection, Chicago
Theological Seminary

Anton Boisen's sister

Boisen's sister, Marie Louise, was all he was not as a child. She was brilliant, spirited, creative, and gregarious. Boisen held a life-long jealousy toward his energetic sister and her excellence in the world of academia, in particular scientific studies. She was a bright and beautiful woman. She was completely unselfish. She received a Bachelor of Science degree from Indiana University in 1900 with a major in the Department of English.[66]

In that same year, Marie married Morton Clark Bradley, who became the Assistant Controller of the Boston and Maine Railroad; and the couple had two children. She lived her adult life in Arlington, Massachusetts. Her religious background under her grandfather's tutelage was New Side Reformed Presbyterian Church. She joined the Presbyterian Church in Massachusetts and was always a faithful attendant. Marie's mother, Elizabeth Louisa Wylie Boisen, came to Arlington to live with her daughter after her own mother and father died.

Marie's daughter, named Louise after her grandmother, graduated from Radcliff College and her son, Morton Clark Jr. was a *cum laude* graduate of the Harvard College class of 1933. In his adult life, he was a nationally known art restorer and collector who was considered the dean of American art restorers in the 1940s and 1950s. The tradition of academic excellence had continued into the next generation.

In her later years, Boisen's mother lost her memory and during the last three years of her life she had vision impairment. In a letter dated January 1925, Louisa thanked Anton signing it "as always with a heart full of love, Mother." In another letter dated October 1926, she thanked Anton for his long and informative letters. She told him of her family life and urged Boisen to write her more news. She said that her eyes were no good.

Morton C. Bradley, Jr., great-grandson of Theophilus and Rebecca Wylie, had a fondness for the Indiana University Art Museum and the Wylie House on Second Street in Bloomington even though he lived his entire life in Arlington, Massachusetts. His mother, Marie Boisen Bradley, grew up in Wylie House and his grandmother, Louisa Wylie Boisen, had lived there for most of her adult life.

Friends of Morton Clark, Jr. remembered him for his brilliant mind. At his death in 2004, he left a portion of his estate to Indiana University naming the Wylie House Museum as one of the recipients. Many photographs that Anton had made during his life time were in the collection. In particular the Assistant Curator at Wylie House let me see a handwritten project of Boisen's entitled, *The Church of the Small Community: It's Problems and Opportunities.* This was a carefully handwritten set of manila individually colored pages with a photograph to go along with the text. They represented research done during the rural survey work for the Presbyterian Church in 1911 and 1912.

4

OPENING ANTON BOISEN'S LIFE JOURNEY

Anton Boisen graduated from Bloomington High School in 1893. His high school days were very difficult as he had a struggle with the sense of estrangement. His personal grounding was not firm in those days. The feeling of estrangement was present in high school and to a greater or lesser degree, throughout his life. He never felt grounded regarding his status with his peers.

Anton enrolled at Indiana University. During college he continued to feel inadequate. He was not "rushed" by fraternities. This was in contrast to his sister, for when she entered Indiana University she was "rushed" vigorously. He was proud of his sister, but she reminded him of his own deficiencies. He always compared her abilities over against what he considered his own deficiencies. He had to force himself to attend social affairs. He went out of a sense of duty.

The Indiana University campus was located on the former Dunn's Meadow just east of the main business district and the Monroe County Court House. The original four buildings are still standing as they were at the turn of the nineteenth century on a wooded area now called Dunn's Woods.

Courtesy: Indiana University Archives
Anton Theophilus Boisen 1897
Indiana University Yearbook, Arbutus

On June 9, 1897, Anton Theophilus Boisen received a Bachelor of Arts degree in German language from Indiana University.[67] He was twenty years old. He did not find a full-time job immediately, so he continued studying languages and psychology at Indiana University and attended the Bible class of his favorite professor, Dr. William Lowe Bryan, at the First Presbyterian Church downtown. Eventually, he did get a job teaching French at Bloomington High School (1898-1900). He also tutored French and German at Indiana University and eventually became an Instructor at the University. These teaching positions lasted two years.

OPENING ANTON BOISEN'S LIFE JOURNEY

Easter Day 1898

CONVERSION

On Easter, 1898, Boisen had a spontaneous religious conversion experience. His adolescence was lonely and filled with sexual maladjustments. He had a struggle with obscenities, a taboo in the family. The brother of his grandfather had inquired of the condition of his soul. This piqued his interest in the inner care of his soul. He wrote, "Meanwhile, I had made an alarming discovery. As I turned the leaves of my Greek dictionary, obscene words would leap out of its pages and hit me in the eye, and so they would leap out of other dictionaries also. It was obvious something was seriously wrong." He was on the cusp of a "tipping point."

Easter was a beautiful day, but though a spontaneous religious conversion experience had occurred, it was followed by black despair. Driven to despondency, he went to his room and threw himself on his knees calling for help. Help came. Something seemed to say to him in words, "don't be afraid to tell." He said that a great burden was lifted and he felt happy for the difficulty was socialized. He felt at one with the Fellowship of the Best. There was hope.[68]

First, he went to talk with his mother, and she understood him. Then later he went to see his friend and mentor Dr. William Lowe Bryan, and talked with him about his experience. One thing stood out in the conversation. Bryan told him it would always be necessary to find ways to control the sexual instincts and that he must look to Christ and to some good woman for help. This made a very special impression on Boisen. It confirmed a view that he was in a struggle with inner forces that were sometimes hostile and sometimes not. The identification of God in his life, salvation, and the love of an idealized "good woman" were factors that would govern his entire life story.

At this time, while in Bloomington, he became deeply interested in the writings of Harvard Professor William James. Professor William Lowe Bryan had introduced him to James's *Principles of Psychology* and *The Varieties of Religious Experience*. Professor James understood religion in terms of its fruit, its outcomes. For him, human existence or nonexistence was not a matter of chance, for the fact that we exist means there is purpose in the universe; and that purpose often finds expression in religious experience. In *The Varieties of Religious Experience* James sought the meaning of religion through study of the abnormal as well as the normal. Professor James's work informed Boisen's own study of mental disorder, and the light it can shed on religious experience.

The second chapter of *The Varieties of Religious Experience* contains James's definition of religion:.

> Religion, therefore, as I now ask you arbitrarily to take it, shall mean for us the feelings, acts, and experiences of individuals in their solitude; so far as they apprehend themselves to stand in relation to whatever they may consider the divine. Since the relation may be moral, physical, or ritual, it is evident that out of religion in the sense in which we take it, theologies, philosophies, and ecclesiastical organizations may grow.
>
> Religion is drawn completely into the sphere of experience.
>
> Religion is one's total reaction upon life. You must go behind the foreground of existence and reach down to that curious sense of the whole residual cosmos as an everlasting presence, intimate or alien, terrible or amusing, loveable or odious which in some degree everyone possesses.[69]

Boisen contended that this everlasting occurrence of a "residual cosmos" existed in each individual as an unending presence of either the intimate or the alien. In his experience, personally and as a professional in a mental hospital, he contended that certain mental disorders are closely related to the religious depths of conversion undergone by ordinary individuals. Such disorders often arise in the midst of life crises when individuals are presented with unrealized possibilities on the one hand and the reality of personal finitude on the other. These overly-stressed individuals often descend into the mental underworld, a place for a gathering together vital energies, the "residual cosmos" in an attempt at restructuring – intimate or alien. At this point these individuals are characterized by noticeable religious concern and often by a sense of mystical recognition.

Boisen believed that the universe had purpose and that there was a place for God and humankind in that universe. He came to believe that he had resolved the century's long struggle to reconcile science and religion. In an article, "The Present Status of William James's Psychology of Religion," printed in *The Journal of Pastoral Care*, Boisen emphasized that the "movement for the clinical training of theological students in many ways represented a return to William James and an attempt to take up where he left off. With him it is believed that sickness of the soul might have religious significance." He proposed "to employ the methods of science to attack the problems involved."[70] Writing in 1953, Boisen challenged those engaged in clinical pastoral education to explore the important territory in which William James had blazed the way to try "to build up a body of organized and tested experience relating to the religious life and the laws that govern it."

His mentor, Dr. William Lowe Bryan, had a theory that Boisen later adapted to the understanding of his own mental illness and his theory of education. Professor Bryan's "Theory of the Plateaus in Learning" stated that in the "acquisition of skill, the curve of progress showed a tendency to strike a certain level and stay there, perhaps to even drop, until suddenly there would come an abrupt upward turn. The explanation was found in the hypothesis that at the point where the dead level is reached some obstruction is encountered and at the point where the sharp upward turn occurs this obstacle is removed and overcome." A similar theory of "overcoming internal resistance" is also found in the writings of Sigmund Freud,[71] but Boisen always gave Dr. Bryan credit for teaching him about the Plateaus of Learning.

The contemporary staff writer for the *New Yorker*, Malcolm Gladwell's *The Tipping Point* (New York: Little Brown & Company, 2002) addresses the moment in an epidemic when a virus reaches critical mass. It's the boiling point. It's the moment on the graph, after a long or short respite, when the line starts to shoot straight upwards. *The Tipping Point* is about change. In particular, it presents a new way of understanding why change so often happens as quickly and as unexpectedly as it does. The "tipping point" is the moment of surprise. For Boisen it was at that moment of his preparation for a Call to a congregation by the Presbyterian Church when suddenly catatonic schizophrenia hit him on the blind side.

This concept is related to William Lowe Bryan's "Plateaus of Learning." Both appeal to anyone who wants to understand the world around them in a different way---anyone who wants a new set of tools for learning. This theory of the "Plateaus of Learning" by Bryan became a perspective on healing for Boisen as he struggled to understand his first hospitalization for mental illness in 1920.

5

YALE, FOREST SERVICE, INTRODUCTION TO THE SCIENTIFIC METHOD

In 1903, Boisen gave up teaching high school French in Bloomington and being an Instructor in the Foreign Language Department of Indiana University, and enrolled at Yale University to study in its new forestry program. Inspiration to study forestry was a legacy his father left him from the early days of roaming the forests of southern Indiana. He did well in his studies, and he received a master's degree in forestry in 1905. During that summer of 1905, he was assigned to the United States Government Department of Agriculture, Forest Service, to work in the field making a plan for a five-thousand acre tract as part of a larger "study of woodlot and forest conditions in southern New Hampshire." He chose this assignment because it put him nearer to Alice. He did meet her and received a chilly reception He remained in New Hampshire until August 1906 when he was transferred to Henry's Lake National Forest Reserve near Yellowstone National Park in Wyoming to work in forest management. In this promotion, he got a raise in salary from $1,000 per year to $1,200 per year.[72]

In May 1907 he was transferred to the national office of the Forest Service in Washington, D.C. to work with Dr. Raphael Zon who was Chief Forester in the Division of Silvics (the care and culture of forest trees). He was to do preliminary study of northern hardwoods in the region of the Northeastern States. In June his project was specified as the "Study of Hickories." In July 1907 he was in Bloomington studying hickories in southern Indiana, then in August and September doing the same in Tennessee. In October he was back to Washington, DC in the national office. Here, again, he worked closely with Raphael Zon. In August 1908 he was promoted to be Forest Assistant under Raphael Zon, but in that month he resigned to prepare for the ministry at Union Theological Seminary in New York City.

Boisen served in the Forest Service from 1905 to 1908.[73] Boisen and J. A. Newlin wrote, "The Commercial Hickories," U.S. Department of Agriculture, Forest Service Bulletin 80.[74]

His life-long friend whom he met while in forestry, Raphael Zon, was an outstanding scientist. He taught Boisen the use of the scientific method and scientific observation. This greatly influenced Boisen's thinking and his research using scientific methods. In *Out of the Depths,* Boisen mentions that his training with Raphael Zon helped him in his approach to pastoral work and in his church survey and research work. Fr. Henri J. M. Nouwen, in an interview with Anton, wrote: "In Raphael Zon, he found a scientist who not only strengthened Boisen's clinical sensitivity, but trained him in the systematic survey. The education of Boisen in which the emphasis was always on the empirical approach, using surveys, questionnaires,, and statistical analysis had shaped a great deal of his later contribution to the field of the psychology of religion."[75] Zon expressed compassion during the times of deep distress that Boisen experienced. Beyond being a dispassionate scientist, Zon was also very passionate and relational, "being-with" Boisen in times when he was "at least nearly psychotic."

Many years later, in a letter to The Reverend Francis McPeak dated September 1940, he wrote regarding Raphael Zon: "In Philadelphia, I had a good visit with my old chief Raphael Zon of the Forest Service, and I found his session on the conservation of our natural resources among the most interesting and valuable."[76]

Boisen wrote regularly to the alumni association at the *Yale Forest School News* to report on activities during his lifetime. On three specific occasions, he mentioned how the experience he obtained at Yale Forestry School and the United States Forest Service helped in his ministry. For example, he wrote in 1947 *Alumni Newsletter*: "My present task seems far-removed from my training in forestry, and yet as I look back, I am impressed with the contribution that training has made to anything I may have been able to do."[77] In 1916 Dr. William Lowe Bryan, now President of Indiana University, called upon Boisen for professional advice in forestry related to the planting for 250 acres of watershed in the Bloomington area.

Boisen had revisited the Forestry School while attending the National Council of Congregational Churches at New Haven; and he reported on his ministry and teaching activities at the mental hospital and with Chicago Theological Seminary. At that time he was temporarily at the home of his sister in Arlington, Massachusetts. Writing many years later in the October 4, 1958, *Yale Forest School News* he comments that "at 82 one tends to look backward rather than forward and my activities are largely confined to a swivel chair in the office where I have spent most of the last 26 years." He reminisces about his students and activities of the past 35 years, then he comments again, "This is a far cry from the Forest School of 1905, but as I look back I see the years I spent at forestry as far from wasted. They have been on the contrary a pre-condition of whatever I may have been able to accomplish." His lengthy and comprehensive case records reflect the precise exactness and scientifically accurate compilation of data that he learned at Forest School. They are indeed sometimes written as if he were plotting out a lot for the study of hickories.

6

CALL TO MINISTRY

During his years at Yale, Boisen got in touch with a renewed longing for matters of the soul. As he was walking down the streets of New Haven in the spring of 1905, he felt a call to ministry. The next day, on April 2, he attended chapel and the President of Union Theological Seminary in New York, The Reverend Henry Sloan Coffin, was preaching at the chapel service. His subject was the "Call to Ministry." This was a synchronistic moment for Boisen, and he felt his own call to ministry being confirmed.

Then he heard another memorable sermon on April 9 in New York by The Reverend Dr. Charles Cuthbert Hall, a graduate of Oberlin College and a former President of Union Theological Seminary. The subject was Abraham's sacrifice of Isaac. Hall's point was that before an individual can enter into fellowship with God, he/she must endure some such test. Boisen's test was another rejection by Alice that he must now endure. He felt dashed to pieces, yet nearer to a decision for his life.[78]

During a visit to Washington, DC, in 1908, while still in the Forestry Service national office, his longing to enter ministry was again challenged by a sermon he heard at the Washington DC

First Congregational Church by the senior pastor, Dr. Samuel H. Woodrow who said in his closing remarks: "If by chance there is someone here tonight who has had a great vision of God's purpose for him and who has been unfaithful to that vision, I call upon him to arise and give himself into the hands of the Great Potter in order that he may be made again another vessel as it seems good unto the Potter." He said the sermon had the effect of driving him almost psychotic. He made a decision to leave the government forestry service and pursue ministry. He felt that God's Providence was leading him.

In 1908, he enrolled at Union Theological Seminary, New York City. At the time of his enrollment Union had a student body of about 170 and a faculty of twelve scholars. Once at Union, he wanted to study pastoral psychology; but there was no one on the faculty teaching that subject. He chose Union because of its scientific approach to theology. He spent his field work experience at Spring Street Presbyterian Church in New York's West Side during his first year. This was his first introduction in the ministry of the social gospel in an urban society. It was a valued experience in a direct "hands on" ministry.

At the beginning of his second year, Dr. George Albert Coe arrived, and he inaugurated the first courses in pastoral psychology offered by an American theological school. He was an eminent theologian and teacher of psychological studies and the ministry. Coe's book, *The Psychology of Religion,* was an important text dealing with a psychological analysis of religion. Coe was particularly interested in the study of religious experience. In the Preface to *The Psychology of Religion*, Professor Coe states that "this work is intended primarily as a handbook for beginners in the psychological analysis of religion. The justification of attempting such a handbook lies partly in the inherent difficulty of analyzing religious experience, and partly in conditions that grow out of the extreme youth of the psychology of religion." [79] The "individualistic" approach of Coe stayed with Boisen, and he developed a dynamic view of the psychology of religion grounded in human behavior and religious experience. Like Coe, he despaired that theologians tended to rely solely on texts rather than the inclusion of human experience. Boisen took every course and seminar that Coe offered at Union.

He did differ with Coe on the importance of the mystical experience in religion. For Boisen faith in the reality of the mystical experience was fundamental. Coe found it questionable. Coe also had an aversion to the pathological and held that the study of pathology lay outside the province of a specialist in religion. Coe was critical of William James and his *Varieties of Religious Experience* (1902).[80] Boisen was to be plunged into the existence of his own and other's pathology in the hospital, and he esteemed greatly William James and his *Varieties of Religious Experience* (1902). Despite these differences, as Boisen explored the borderland between religious experience and mental illness, he considered Coe one of his staunchest supporters.[81] However, Boisen admits that he got through Union Seminary without knowing that Pierre Janet, or Sigmund Freud or Adolph Mayer[82] existed.

Coe made a significant impression on Boisen. He considered Coe to be one of the great minds in the psychology of religion, along with William James, Stanley Hall, Edwin Starbuck, and James Pratt.[83] Coe believed that any good pastor exploring the psychology of religion cannot afford to neglect his or her own psychological dimension.

Union was then a center of the Social Gospel movement and liberal theology and politics.[84] Union was on the threshold of a new era in theological education. The Socialist Democratic Party politician Norman Thomas graduated with Boisen at Union. At

Union, Thomas had become a Socialist.[85] Thomas was ordained a Presbyterian minister in 1911, and he ministered to a Protestant church in New York's East Harlem. Thomas was an opponent of World War I, and a founder of the American Civil Liberties Union. Thomas was its presidential candidate in 1928, 1932, and 1936.

Boisen got a good dose of the Social Gospel liberalism of his day, and he carried that zeal into the parish life later. Boisen's files at Chicago Theological Seminary contained a photo of the 1911 Union Seminary graduating class with his dear friend Reverend Fred Eastman.

Courtesy Hammond Library Boisen Collection CTS
Union Seminary Class of 1911
Anton Boisen, Norman Thomas, Ned Kennedy, and Fred Eastman noted

At Union, he also had an opportunity to take theology

courses with Dr. William Adams Brown, perhaps the ablest liberal theologian of the time. Brown was a Presbyterian, educated at Yale University (B.A., 1886), Union Theological Seminary (1890), and the University of Berlin (1890-92). Dr Brown was Roosevelt Professor of Systematic Theology at Union Theological Seminary during the time Boisen was enrolled. Brown's *Christian Theology in Outline* (1906) was a primary source for liberal theology at Union Seminary. Boisen was influenced by the empirical theology that Brown upheld. Boisen thus became conversant with the liberal theology of his day.[86] Liberal theologians of this period used insights and methods from the social sciences, psychology, and the late nineteenth century and early twentieth century liberal theological movement to shape Christian thought. Boisen viewed himself as one who wished to relate traditional theology and contemporary thought.[87] Later in life, he spoke of his years at Union as being the best years of his life.

In 1911, Boisen graduated from Union with honors having a cumulative grade point average of 93. In that same year, he was ordained a Presbyterian minister by the Presbytery of Brookline, Newton Centre, Massachusetts.[88] Later he ministered within the Congregational Church because that is where opportunity first opened for him. He referred to himself as a "Presbygationalist."[89]

7

COUNTRY CHURCH SURVEY

In 1911, Boisen and his seminary friend, The Reverend Fred Eastman, became Field Investigators for Country Church Work supported by the Presbyterian Church's Board of Home Missions of the Department of Church and Country Life.[90] He began his ministry spending a year and a half making surveys under the direction of The Reverend Warren H. Wilson.

Wilson was the most important individual in early twentieth century life and rural church reform.[91] For Wilson, the frontier was no longer geographical. The frontier was sociological.[92] Boisen and Eastman joined what became the largest and most important rural sociological survey(s) of the early twentieth century.[93] Rural America was changing, and the goal of the surveys was to illuminate more clearly the orientation and perceptions not only of the rural church, but also the perceptions and biases of the reformers.

The school and the church were the sources of security for the life of the rural community. The schools changed fairly rapidly, but the churches stood steadfast in the center of the village or "snuggled in the vales."[94] From 1900 to 1920, more Americans became aware of rural conditions and problems than at any other time in its history.

Anton Boisen and Eastman traced the growth of minor religious sects, which stress direct conversion experiences. They made a three-month rural survey in Missouri locally under the supervision of Rev. William Templeton, pastor of the Presbyterian Church in Kirksville, Missouri, and Professor John R. Kirk of the Normal School at Kirksville. They were sent to Ethel, Missouri to survey three counties in the northeast part of the state and made a thorough record of the churches in the three counties remarking "that they were impressed when they first arrived on the field by the freedom and naturalness with which people, men as well as women, spoke on religious themes. On the whole, the attitude toward religion showed little denominational strife."[95] This was a contrast to what Boisen experienced in the various denominational strivings in Bloomington as a boy.

In northeastern Missouri "the breakdown according to religious membership was about 56 per cent Roman Catholic and 23 percent Protestant. Ninety-two percent of the Protestant churches had a minister at least one time per month." He described the circuit rider system among these country churches in the early part of the twentieth century. The minister came and spent the day with worship two times on Sunday. The minister stayed until the next day. The Circuit Rider System was predominant within the Methodist Church in pioneer America.

"The average minister to a country church lived in some nearby town and had four country charges, one of which he visited each Sunday. Very few of these ministers had horse and buggies. Their charges were so far apart that that means of conveyance would have been useless."[96] In the *Summary,* Boisen wrote: "The ministers live where they do not preach and they preach where they do not live." He went on to point out that the churches prefer it this way.

The members of the congregations could visit around, and it was cheaper and the responsibilities were lighter. In Boisen's time the existing custom of the ministers was to live in the towns, where their own advantages were the greatest, and to expect country churches to support them.

He makes a distinction between the *preacher* and the *pastor*. Few of the preachers make pastoral visits among their people in the country. However, the successful country ministers throughout the United States live with their people. "The work of a pastor is far more effective in the saving of souls and the building of churches than the work of a preacher. Under the present stress and strain the leadership of the pastor is sorely needed in the country community, where none, as a rule, reside who do not have to work twelve hours a day."[97]

Besides this critical difference between the ministry of the preacher and the pastor, the report raised several issues regarding the need for socialization in the community. The social center was often the country store, or the Sunday morning church community in Sullivan County, Missouri. Today, one can visit in the "crags and hollers" of Missouri or Southern Indiana, where Boisen grew up; and find a country store like these.

ANTON THEOPHILUS BOISEN:

Courtesy: Hammond Library Boisen Collection CTS
**One center of social life in rural America in the period
of Boisen's research was often the country store with its
wooden porch and barrel benches.**

For social interaction, the country store played its important
role in bringing men and women together informally. It was here
that the farmers met to swap yarns and exchanged views on crops
and the weather, on politics, and on religion. Especially on Saturday
afternoon and evening, the farmers and their wives and children
came to town in large numbers to go to the country stores to shop
and swap stories.

Out of Boisen's Social Gospel Theology, he highlighted social
service to the poor. The Social Gospel was a rethinking of the
Christian religious ideal of love in the light of the modern science
and modern social life. For many, life in American society, in
particular those in urban areas, where the mass of immigrants came
to settle in the mid nineteenth century, theirs was too often many
lives of doom, despair, and degradation. Through the use of

scientific methodology, the Social Gospel movement showed what part the environment played in molding the character for good or evil, and it showed also how environment can be changed. Country researchers were most concerned about the state of country schools. The major targets of the people who made the surveys were schools and churches, two institutions that loomed large in rural society because there were so few others.

The hardship of the poor was a major social issue in these rural counties of Missouri. Neither the social lodges nor the churches met the essential needs of the deprived in the county.

To extend the membership of the church among the small farm owners and among the hired hands and tenant farmers, who constitute about 15 percent of the country population, was a great task for the church. For Boisen, "the hope of the church is with the poor man. He has the experience that begets religion. His life is made up of the simple elements which enter into all human experience. And he has no other disturbing factor. He provides the warmth and passion of religious feeling. The future of the church as a religious institution is bound up with her relation to the men who work the land."

He went on to highlight the need for improving the schools. All of the country schools were one room schools, cross-lighted, unventilated buildings. There was no industrial training, and the teachers were poorly paid. Very few of them had slate blackboards and not one had an indoor toilet.

The Circuit Rider and Three-Hour-a-Month surveys showed vividly that the great need was for pastors to live in the country in order to develop the church clubs and societies it needed to help bring individuals into the church.

Later in his theological writings, Boisen described bringing people into the church, and how vital this was to the life of the believer. Throughout his life and ministry, he always felt that "sociality" of individuals was very important. Sociality is a term from the writings of George Herbert Mead who was very important in Boisen's developmental concepts. "Churches who face the future with courage and concentration will build manses for the ministers, and when this is done it will be possible to retain in the country serviceable and useful men."[98] Boisen and Eastman pointed out in their reports that change and reform in the rural church will demand sacrifice.

Boisen continued, "It may even mean that some churches will have to die, but long ago the church's Master died that others might live. Is the church afraid to follow His example? Will some churches be willing to die for the salvation of their community? It may mean that some ministers must give up their homes in the towns to take up a two-acre patch of ground beside a country church to live and work and die there among people who do not appreciate or understand. But the Kingdom of God will come nearer. Is that worth while?"[99] This is an example of the zeal and courage Boisen put into his survey work for the Presbyterian Church.

Later, Boisen went to western Tennessee and made another rural survey, this time alone, in Gibson County.[100] The study drew on published reports, county records, and personal visits to parts of the county. Again, as in the earlier study with Fred Eastman, Boisen sought out informed and public figures in the community for feedback. He visited approximately thirty families in the county for detailed inquiry. He then, as in his forestry days, used "sample plots" or areas of the county for intensive study. In all, twenty-one "sample plots" were studied. Boisen comments that he received a hearty dose of Southern hospitality from the individuals within Gibson County. The county was predominantly agricultural, although there were some small box and basket factories and a dwindling lumbering business in the area. Cheap labor made from 75 cents to $1.25 a day in pay.

The African Americans lived for the most part in small houses of less than three rooms generally unpainted. Many settlements were back from the main highway, some of which could be reached only by opening a number of gates.

The African American church was a vital part of their identity and their community. In most southern areas in the early part of the 20th century, the churches were outside the town limits. The African American was often blamed for petty thievery, drunkenness, and stealing; but when Boisen pressed individuals who were derogatory toward the African Americans, he discovered that they never knew an African American who would steal. The cases fell flat. Almost 66% of the African Americans in 1911 could read and write.

A major concern for the churches was the question of what the church was doing for the poor people of the county, as had been his challenge in his survey work in Missouri. The five largest Protestant denominations were the Baptist, Methodist, Cumberland Presbyterian, Disciples of Christ, and Southern Presbyterian. Throughout Gibson County the church was strongly entrenched in the affections of the people. The churches, along with the schools, were the great institutions of the area. The usual complaints of country life in the small church were not prevalent in Gibson County.

Boisen made nine practical recommendations:
1. The preacher or pastor ought to speak the language of the country.
2. He ought "to be able to heal the hurts" of the people
3. The church ought to be open to lectures on good farming.
4. While the young like to play, this is not wicked. They ought to be encouraged from the church.

5. The church and the homes of its members ought to be open for the sociality[101] of the life in the "Fellowship of the Best."

6. The church ought to support the organization of the farmer for better income for the purpose of taking care of his own business and for the protection of his homework of the farm

7. He recommended the "great Sunday School movement."

8. He recommended a building movement in the country churches in Gibson County in which there shall be rooms erected for the teaching of religion.

9. He recommended that there be a "new kind of school" established for "grown-up folks." It should be a religious school, full of sound hymns and beginning every class with prayer. This school would focus on the church and the farm community.

His strong recommendation was for "religious based" education to be provided to the farmer, something similar to the extension programs that the Morrill Land Grant colleges of 1862, provided throughout the U.SA.

He concluded, "If we can keep our church people in the country, we can keep up the churches that are there. If the farmers prosper and are happy there, we will have preachers to live with them. If the schools turn their hand to making good farmers, there will be no great trouble about maintaining the church in the country."[102] After this survey in Tennessee was completed, he returned to Missouri and to the Salt River Presbytery to do surveys.

During 1911 and 1912, Boisen and Eastman produced important records regarding how social, economic, and demographic changes had affected the rural church in America. As early as 1916, Anton Boisen in an article in the *American Journal of Sociology* titled, "Factors which have to do With the Decline of the Country Church 1916," highlighted some of the specific problems. Boisen was particularly interested in how change impacted church attendance, as well as school training, financial standing, social activities and outreach in compassionate care for the neighbor. Boisen's statistics on the rural church showed him how the breakdown of traditional authority destroys popular and other pertinent questions. A couple of conclusions drawn from this study were vital in his later ministry.

One conclusion, drawn from the studies of churches in Missouri, Tennessee, Kansas, New York, and Maine, that later became a shaping vision for Boisen in his ministry in mental health, was the importance of the church's task in the care of the soul and the sociality of the individual.

First, "Cannot the hell of wrong habit, of diseased will, of misused opportunity, and of guilty conscience, be made as real and just as the hell pictured by the early Puritan preacher? Cannot the necessity of membership in and loyalty to the organization in which men and women are associated at their highest level be made just as convincing as the old doctrine of salvation though the taking out of life insurance in the church, accepting a creed, attending worship, and partaking of the sacraments?"[103] To make these traditional moral virtues of habit, will, opportunity, and soul-care of primary importance to the individual was a major theme later in his work as an educator and chaplain to the mentally ill. His concern, at this time, and as a recurring concern in his later ministry as a chaplain, was the failure of the major Protestant churches to meet the everyday needs of individuals.

Second, in a later article, "In Defense of Mr. Bryan, a Personal Confession of a Disciple of Dr. Fosdick," Boisen came to the conclusion that, from his studies of 12,000 individuals in five different regions of the United States, wherever the liberal influence is strongest, there the influence of the church tended to be the weakest. This was true in conservative Tennessee, where they were still holding debates in the country school houses as to how a person should be baptized. The Church influence was least in those sections where people had begun to think and question and where liberal ideas had banished the old fear of future punishment and the old faith in a vicarious atonement, which in Tennessee and Missouri and even in Kansas still prevailed. "The old message has lost its power and the liberal message is still without the element of conviction and authority and emotional earnestness that characterized the old appeal. It is a situation that was well calculated to fill with deep concern those who believe in the church and in those things that the church represents."[104]

The method of theological investigation he promoted in the rural life study was later transformed into research into the life stories of individuals in crisis in the mental hospital setting, as well as in other areas of pastoral ministry. Out of this research came a method and model for doing theological learning that would become groundbreaking in the second quarter of the twentieth century.

8

IOWA STATE COLLEGE AND TWO
PARISH MINISTRIES

After a year and a half in survey work, Boisen felt that he wanted to enter the parish ministry. In the fall of 1912, he accepted a call as college chaplain for the Congregational Church's ministry at Iowa State College in Ames, Iowa.[105] However, college campus ministry did not endear itself to him. He wrote in *Out of the Depths*, about the Iowa State College experience. "I was to live at the College, getting acquainted with students and faculty and using the resources of the College in the service of a nearby country church. But I went there in a state of mind little favorable to successful work."[106] He left before a full year was completed.

His grandmother died in 1913 just two months before her 101st birthday, so he went back to Bloomington to help with the family plans of making arrangements for the Wylie homestead at 307 Second Street. Two of Grandmother Wylie's grandchildren made the house available for rent for two years, and then it was sold to Professor Amos Hershey in 1915. Professor Hershey was a member of the Political Science faculty. At his death, Dr. Hershey's widow sold the house to Indiana University in 1947, but the Trustees agreed to let her continue to live in it until 1951.

We find Boisen next in the Congregational Church in Wabaunsee, Kansas. There is a fascinating story about this church. It was called "The Beecher Bible and Rifle Church." The church was built in 1847 by a group of Abolitionists from New Haven, Connecticut who came out to help rid Kansas of slavery in a very volatile time of pre-Civil war conflict over admitting Kansas and/or Nebraska as slave states. Each of the founding fathers of the congregation had been given a Bible and a Sharpe rifle supplied from The Reverend Henry Ward Beecher's church in Brooklyn, New York.

Boisen stayed in Wabaunsee two years. During his tenure there was a renewal of interest in the church life. He started an experiment in rural development. Boisen organized the people to build sidewalks, improve the churchyard and the cemetery, and to better the economic and social lives of the people of the rural community. He might have stayed longer; however, eventually his involvement in a number of social action groups ran cross grain with the conservative religious community. He did gain the attention of the Extension Service at Kansas State College of Agriculture only a few miles away where he met The Reverend Arthur Holt, pastor of the Congregational Church in Manhattan, Kansas with whom he collaborated to develop several social outreach programs in the rural community. Along with the college, they promoted a health clinic, play festivals, excellent lectureships, and farm demonstrations by specialists. He noted in his autobiography, "I left after two years feeling that all was a failure, but taking with me one thing of crucial importance in the years that have followed the friendship of Rev. Arthur Holt"[107] Holt was to play an important part in his becoming a seminary professor later in his career.

In his next pastorate in North Anson, Maine (1916 to 1917), he was very active again in an effort to involve the members of the congregation in a ministry for those with special needs. He focused on the development of programs for outreach to the community. He was up at the crack of dawn and into these programs for the community, but he was viewed as a threat to the other church in town, and his own church began to back away. Boisen did not relate on a close one-to-one basis with individuals, families, and the groups in the church; but he wrote that he was not thrown out of this church; however, there was little gain.[108] Nevertheless, one thing he had learned was that it was better to be a patient and good listener and live-with-the-people before you began to center attention on social programs and outreach in their community.

World War I

Then came WW I. He applied for a position as Secretary for the YMCA with the American Expeditionary Forces in France. From 1917 to1919, he was assigned to a machine-gun battalion of the First Division's Sixteenth Infantry, which was the same regiment his mother's grandfather, Richard Dennis, had commanded in the War of 1812. Then he was transferred to the Forty Second Battalion, a battalion from the state of Indiana where he met some of his friends from Indiana University. Boisen was with the Allied forces under the command of French General Foch and later General Pershing, marching with them to the Rhine. Boisen was in the last major offensive as the American forces were fighting at Chateau-Thierry from May 31 to July 10, 1918, near Belleau Wood, then at the Battle of Saint-Mihiel southeast of Verdun from September 12 to the 16th, 1918, and the Meuse-Argonne offensive from September 26, 1918 to November 11, 1918. The Meuse-Argonne was the last major engagement of World War I. It was the biggest operation and bloodiest victory of the American Expeditionary Force in the War.

After the Armistice, when the Forty Second left for home, he went with his former chief, The Reverend Warren Wilson, to start a school for American soldiers not far from Coblenz in Germany.[109] He taught a history course and met a German forester. They took the students to visit old Roman front-lines and Roman watchtowers, visiting a castle on the Rhine. After about ten days, he got into difficulty when the American commanding general, Johnson Hagood, suspected him of teaching the boys German forestry. He could teach all the French or American forestry he wanted, but absolutely no German forestry.[110] Such was a general sentiment immediately after WW I.

In July 1919, he returned to the United States, and became, for a year, the State Supervisor for the North Dakota Rural Survey of the Interchurch World Movement of North America. This organization emerged on the horizon as suddenly as a meteor. Their goal was the "evangelization of the world for Christ in this generation." John R. Mott served as Chair of the Executive Committee.

Robert Eliot Speer[111] of the Presbyterians was cautious, troubled by what he called the pell-mell character of the Interchurch World Movement. When the organization did not meet budget, it was financially backed by John D. Rockefeller, Jr. who was an enthusiastic advocate of the interdenominational agency that would bring to Protestantism the kind of efficiency his father's Standard Oil venture had brought to the country. Despite financial backing from the Rockefellers, the investment of major Protestant churches waned. Several major denominations questioned its ambitions and its lack of clarity of purpose. By 1920 the Interchurch World Movement Organization had failed. There was much disillusion and dissension, and it collapsed before it completed its planned survey work.[112] The failure of the Interchurch Movement led to discouragement and despair among many Protestant leaders. The final direction of the major Protestant churches was to strengthen the uniting of the churches within the Federal Council of Churches of Christ in America. Boisen came back to New England and moved to Arlington, Massachusetts to live temporarily with his sister and her family. He did not engage in church surveys again.

Major Difficulties in the Parish Ministry

In the Kansas and Maine pastorates, Boisen had four major difficulties: (1. He was a scientific researcher and a coordinator who had trouble relating to human beings on an emotional level. As Henry Nouwen wrote, "Boisen approached his parish more as a forest that needed a survey than as a pasture that needed a shepherd."[113] (2. On his own admission, he was a bad preacher; (3. He found that his seminary preparation and experience in rural survey did not prepare him for the day-to-day personal experience of living among the joys and woes of people in the congregations; (4. He, most of all, tried to push the Social Gospel on rural churches that were not ready for that form of applied and progressive Christianity. In those kinds of situations, it was necessary to spend time building personal relationships before proposing social action programs. "There is no greater peril to the rural church than the up-to-date reformer who looks at something that has been there for centuries and suddenly finds that it is all wrong."[114]

There is a story that the renowned rural social reformer Edmund Brunner told in his autobiography. It is about a meeting in the village of Phelps, New York, a small, friendly community of approximately100 residents. He was an advocate for the Social Gospel. He came from Manhattan to report on the diagnosis and recommendations to the congregation of a recent survey. After he had finished, a white haired gentleman rose to offer the closing prayer. It was brief and to the point, "Dear Lord" he said, "Thou knowest that we have heard many new and strange things this night, but we thank Thee that Thou art the same yesterday, today, and forever. Amen." Whereupon, he stomped out.[115] Boisen encountered that point of view in many of his parish adventures. Boisen can be given credit for trying, but he failed to do well in the congregational ministry. He ran into difficulty finding a suitable opening. He was no longer considered by the Congregational Church for further ministry. Therefore in 1920 he turned to his original denominational affiliation with the Presbyterians, being helped in this by his former pastor in Bloomington who was now an executive at the national level of the Presbyterian Church.

Throughout this period, Boisen's seminary friend, Rev. Fred Eastman, was a close comrade and associate. In 1920, during the dark days of his first major mental breakdown and hospitalization, Eastman was with him giving support personally or writing letters that were encouraging to Boisen when he was in "the depths." In his autobiography, *Out of the Depths*, Boisen cites twelve extensive letters exchanged with Fred Eastman between 1920 and 1923. These letters represent Boisen's trust in Eastman as they contain the profound depths of his struggle with mental illness. He said that Eastman was, for him, a representative of psychotherapy at its best. Eastman was not a trained counselor, but he was skilled in interpersonal relationships nurturing understanding and friendship on one side and trust on the other.[116]

The effort to return to the pastorate, however, ended in the midst of what became a year-long hospitalization for catatonic schizophrenia. We will return to this hospitalization, but we need to now give attention to the "love of his life," the elusive Alice Batchelder who was living in Chicago and working in a bank.

9

THE ELUSIVE ALICE BATCHELDER

Courtesy Hammond Library, CTS
Alice Batchelder
To the Memory of A. L. B.

"For her sake, I understood the adventure out of which this book has grown. Her compassion upon a wretch in direst need, her wisdom and courage and unswerving fidelity have made possible the measure of success which may have been achieved. To her I dedicate it in the name of Love which would surmount every barrier, and bridge every chasm, and make sure the foundations of the universe."

ANTON THEOPHILUS BOISEN:

The Exploration of the Inner World

This was the dedication to Alice Batchelder in his first major book, *The Exploration of the Inner World,* published in 1936, one year after her death. Running through Boisen's life, since his post college days in Bloomington, was his love for Alice Batchelder. He met her in 1902 when she was a YWCA worker on the Indiana University campus. She was a recent graduate of Smith College. Alice was 22 years old and he was 25. She was the girl of his dreams. Never had he been so attracted. He was riveted. Her presence filled him with a heightened sense of himself. He wanted to participate in the power of her love that both energized him and frightened him.

He fell in love with her, and it was a love that swept him off his feet. However, he received no encouragement. He could not forget her even though they were separated for extended periods of time. He had a deep feeling that his very existence was involved in this love for Alice. The thought of her took possession of him, and he experienced intense longing and yearning for her the rest of his life. In fact, throughout his long life, Alice Batchelder was a figure in the shadows, a dream never realized. He wrote in *Out of the Depths*: "Through her, I was led into the Christian ministry; and with the passing of the years my love for her has become more and more interwoven with my religious faith."[117] In the end, Alice was very much affiliated with his idea of God and his journey toward the saving grace of God. In his adventure with/without Alice, he was defined by a power greater than himself, and yet he knew that he never had been so truly himself as when connected to her presence

Boisen and Alice had an on and off "acquaintance"[118] through letters and occasional meetings, until her death in 1935. She refused his many proposals of marriage. I wonder what would have happened to Boisen if Alice had ceased all contact with him from the beginning. Or, on the other hand, what might have been his professional career direction if they had married? The answer to these two questions is only idle speculation. Instead there was an association that continued until her death, until his death. She represented a mysterious, mediumistic, figure who never became a *real person*. In his autobiography, *Out of the Depths*, written when he was 82, there is hardly a page on which he does not refer to her and his love for her.

In the diary he kept from about 1917 until the early 1960s, he mentioned Alice regularly. For example, he made references to Alice in his *1924 Diary*. They were short and uninformative. "I received a letter from Alice today just as I was about to send her a telegram." April 1l, "Went to Alice's tonight. She had a leg injury that was much better." On April 13, "Wrote to Alice today an important letter." Then on April 29, "I wrote to Alice today. Her letter in return was of general information." On May 17 he wrote, "Had a futile attempt at a letter to Alice." On August 31, "Wrote today to Alice a very important letter, and most of the day was consumed with this." On September 6 he wrote, "Yet another letter to Alice." On November 27 he entered in his diary: "Wrote today a very important letter to Alice." This unreciprocated love was certainly a major factor in his deep lifetime of sadness.

Alice died in 1935. At her death, he felt a letting go, surrender to his own identity and formation as an educator, chaplain, and more and more, a writer. For the many years he saw her and dreamed of her, he was dependent upon her. She was a sounding board for his thoughts, if not his feelings. There was a form of transference with Alice that kept Boisen going. The thought of her let him know that he was not totally isolated. Fr. Henri J. M. Nouwen wrote about

Alice: "She is life, the curing authority, to which the patient becomes more and more attached but who is also able to make him more and more aware of his attachment in such a way that he is slowly able to develop a more independent, mature relationship."[119]

Upon returning to the East from North Dakota in 1920, there was an invitation to come to Alice's to meet her family, that being her sister Anne and their friend Catherine Wilson.[120] This would be the first time he had seen her in nine years. He spent a delightful evening in Alice's home.

Afterwards, he sent a typed letter to Alice in which he set forth stridently his love for her. July 24, 1920, he wrote: "First of all, I would express the deepening conviction that has resulted from the brief visit in your home that the faith that has guided me all these years is indeed right. For I know now, as I have never known before, that I love you and that I will always love you and that I would rather have even just your friendship than the love of any other woman in the world." He goes on in the next paragraph to acknowledge a letter she has written to him that he interpreted as "entering upon a new period" in their relationship. He looked to the future and was now planning for it with confidence and hope. He also included in his letter a statement asking her to receive him into her fellowship. Then he pulled out all the stops, and wrote "for that to me is the Kingdom of God on earth. Without that my faith remains unsupported, and I am a wanderer without." He then made a striking statement that tells us much about the source of his inner strength as a man and as a professional. "I would ask also *Your* blessing and *Your* commission *without which I cannot speak with authority or with power.* I believe this, and I feel that it is very difficult for me to take another step until *You* have done what this involves."[121] On several occasions in this letter, Boisen capitalizes the word "You" when it is referring to Alice.[122] Unconsciously she is beginning to represent the Holy to him. This will become more apparent later.

Nothing was to come from this exchange. She wrote him a letter soon after this encounter calling off another visit to her home. She wrote:

"I am going to call off the visit tonight because of Miss Wilson's not being very well; but I want also to speak to you at this time about your stay in Chicago. I think you have misinterpreted my dinner invitation by reading into it more than I put there. I understood your letter to say you would be passing through Chicago, and it seemed a simply friendly act to invite you to dinner, to give you a chance to see me as you had asked and to let you get a glimpse of me in my setting, so to speak. But that did not mean, as you seem to have concluded, that I am going to keep on seeing you frequently, or go out with you or make such a radical change in my attitude as that would imply. There could be no question of such a thing as your going on our vacation with us. Your knowledge of plain human nature, to say nothing of my nature, should tell you things cannot be forced like that."

Then she finished in another tone, "I am glad you came to dinner and glad we have seen each other, but for the present that must suffice"[123] In this exchange, Alice was frankly stating her feelings and her attitude toward Boisen in a way that was clear and strong, something Boisen would not accept from her. And it is understandable as she does and she doesn't cut him off in this communication and this invitation to have a visit in her home. My hunch is that the words *"for the present* this must suffice"* would be heard positively by Boisen.

Later in the summer, she wrote this brusque note: "My Dear *Mr. Boisen*, I can have no other answer for you than the one which is and always has been final. Our ways must be apart; it cannot be otherwise. With good wishes for your future work. Alice L.

Batchelder." They had no contact for another ten years.

Despite the long periods of absence and Alice's refusal of his offer of love, he was in love, he was *in* love. Wherever he went, he saw her lively form, her beautiful full visage, and her gentle eyes. He heard her soft voice and felt her look upon him, longingly. That always made him blush to the roots of his hair. He wanted to spend his life with her.

Despite all of the discouraging messages and events in their lives, Boisen did see Alice Batchelder on a somewhat regular basis while he was teaching at Chicago Theological Seminary. They would go out for dinner, to the theatre, and to the opera. In his autobiography he mentions that in 1928 and 1929 they met about every other week and during other times as he was able to find occasion. She seemed to come close to saying she loved him, but stopped short despite his many gestures of love toward her. They had entered into what he called a "covenant of friendship" on Thanksgiving day in 1929; and for the first time she became able to sign a letter, "With real affection, Alice"[124] They saw each other several times after Thanksgiving Day before he returned to Worcester, but the "covenant of friendship" was viewed differently by Alice than by Boisen. She did not want to pursue a romantic relationship with him. He did toward her.

Thinking back on Easter day 1898 in the midst of anxiety, unhappiness, and depression he felt a great relief and happiness when something seemed to say to him almost in words, "Don't be afraid to tell." Easter day 1905, seven years later, Alice was becoming the way to reach the next "plateau" in his life. He said: "I realized that my love for Alice was really a cry for salvation, and an appeal to a beloved person stronger than myself."[125] Glen Asquith, Jr. wrote in his doctoral dissertation. "Devotion to Alice kept Boisen on course in his desire to stay in the ministry. Some years later being advised to go back into the social studies, he opted to go to another church," saying 'I could not give up the hope of redeeming myself in Alice's' eyes.'"[126]

He received a letter from Alice on August 2, 1935 indicting that she was going to retire and was to have an operation for cancer. She did not want him to visit her or send mementoes of any kind. He began to feel remorseful and guilty that he had not done more to be of help to her. He wrote in his Diary: "What poor use I had made of our friendship, failing in these later years to reach the deeper levels of understanding. And now she was leaving!"[127] Again, Boisen's guilty conscience that was out of proportion to the actual reality for Alice had asked him long ago to leave her alone. Boisen entertained an exceedingly negative concept of himself as a failure, and he was disconsolate now that he had this message and throughout much of his life.

In the midst, Boisen dealt with his sadness by going into another one of his episodes of mental illness. This time he was admitted to the Sheppard and Enoch Pratt Hospital in Baltimore on November13, 1935. He said there were two reasons for this admission. First, his book *Exploration of the Inner World* had not received a favorable contract with a publisher, and, second, there was Alice's imminent death.

He was in the hospital on the second of December 1935 when Alice died. This time the mental illness cleared up within a short period of time; but he had missed the one event he regretted not being able to attend, the Memorial Service for Alice. The last two episodes of hospitalization came at times when strong women in his life died, and he sought to deal with his own feelings by getting sick.

His hospital record shows that he was first focused on the Family of Four. He said that his relationship this time was that he was on top, whereas formerly he was on the bottom. His ideas centered on this family of four: the weak accepting from the strong. He felt it was time for the weak to do something for the strong. He classified himself as the weak one. He thought that the informant was Jesus, and that Jesus had betrayed him. Then he was John the Baptist, and he believed that Lucifer was really John the Baptist. He identified himself as being Mary Magdalene. This kind of ideation lasted for a few days, but he had a speedy recovery this time: Admission was on November 13, 1935 and he was discharged December 16, 1935. The discharge notation by the psychiatrist was "Recovered." He was picked up by his friend Fred Eastman.

About six months after his discharge, Boisen wrote to Alice Batchelder's friend Catherine Wilson, asking that she try to clarify "the situation" for him. It seemed that he had left a document with Catherine Wilson and Alice's sister Anne regarding his perspective on their (Alice and Anton's) relationship. He claimed that Alice had approved publishing this document when both were out of the way. His desire was that the two have some clarity regarding what seemed to him their misapprehension of the relationship.[128]

He wrote: "You will see, for one thing, that our relationship has not been without certain elements of mutual commitment. Alice, in 1907, virtually pledged me her support in my purpose of studying for the ministry. She made me no promise. What she said at the close of the prayer she offered in my behalf, and as she gave me her hand, 'God's promises always come true.' And she stood ready to back that up." All through the years at Union Seminary they corresponded, and she saw him at the end of the third year.

He believed she did not choose to be at his side because during those years he had been "childish and fretful under the discipline to which she rightly subjected me and lacking in true understanding, and this culminated in a particularly tragic failure to rise to the opportunity on the expedition which we made together after my flowers in April of 1919. Her decision that our friendship brought happiness to neither of us and must be broken off was fully justified." He believed he was an object of pity. In a self aggrandized moment he writes that he felt responsible for her losing a job at Lowell as well. She had said she was interested in him and his career, but he understood this to be deeper than she ever intended.

He continued in the letter to put himself down again, claiming her decision to be mysterious was entirely justified. He wrote, "I now see the end and meaning of my life and for which, if my interpretation is correct, her life has been sacrificed. Everything was for me staked upon the faith in my love for her. That faith was one with the faith in the task to which I was committed." He conveyed a vivid picture of himself as one who had ventured to climb some great mountain and who hung suspended in midair, unable without some validation of the faith that had led him, to find any footing or any refuge. "I was ready to grasp at anything, ready to be satisfied with any response which would permit me to feel that connections were established so as she refused this, she left me no alternative but to continue to try to become in some degree worth while."

He continued to tell of what happened after his first psychotic episode and was released from Westboro in 1922, writing letters regularly. Then in the spring of 1925 he went to Chicago, and she refused to see him. It was on the return from Chicago that he stopped off in New York and Boston to look for students for his first CPE group.

He told of meeting a brilliant and attractive young woman who was now the Director of the Council for Clinical Training (Helen Flanders Dunbar). In 1928, Alice consented to see Dunbar and Boisen, and when Helen could not make the trip, he went on anyway. He felt that Alice tried to save him from a relationship with Flanders Dunbar. Alice and Boisen remained friends, but she did not give him her full attention because, now, there was a shadow between the two of them, Anton and Alice. That shadow was Flanders Dunbar.

Probably the closest Boisen ever got to intimacy was with Flanders Dunbar. This occurred on one occasion while he was helping her translate the German text of Eugen Kahn's *Psychopathic Personalities*, and on another, when he was psychotic in 1930 and Dunbar spent some time with him in his seclusion room. Boisen was no longer psychotic by the time she left the ward.[129]

When he moved to Elgin, he did not feel Alice gave him confidence as she had previously done. He lamented that his love for her had been imperfect and even to the end he felt he had failed to bring to her the comfort and support it should have been his privilege to express. "What profit is it, if we are able to even move mountains and have not loved?"

He felt, to the end, that Alice's own attitude was due to the alleged requirement that he should *prove* the strength and genuineness of his love for her. He asked Catherine Wilson to chose whether the sentence was exile, representing failure as a friend and lover and the impossibility now of doing anything about it. In the face of the door that was shut. "I can only bow my head in deepest sorrow."[130]

He ended this long and detailed letter with these words: "This question I cannot answer. I can be sure only of one thing, that I believe in my love for Alice as one with the love that is eternal and that in what is left to me of this life it shall be my steady purpose to make her influence an increasing source of power and inspiration to become in some measure worthy of her."[131] There is no evidence that there was a response.

His self-blaming was very evident in this letter. There was a pervading sense of unworthiness about his personhood. This went back into his early childhood rearing, before and during, his sojourn in the household of his grandfather Theophilus Adam Wylie. It was a practice of self abasement that he wanted to get rid of, but he never fully accomplished it.

His letters and communication reveal some of the inner dynamic of the man in relation to a woman. He was at once assertive and deferential, hopeful and saddened, in reality and in fantasy. I believe that a major precipitating factor for his mental illness and hospitalized in 1920, 1930, and 1935 had to do with his struggle to find a significant relationship with one woman, Alice Batchelder. After 1935, and the death of Alice, he had only one brief episode near his own death, but essentially no further major episodes of mental illness.

With Alice, Boisen was prey to joy and agony at one and the same time. Sometimes he felt as if his heart was so full and over flowing that it would burst, and then he would fall stricken on the floor for all to see and wonder, what could have befallen this man. He felt an overwhelming desire to confess, to unburden himself, to pour out his inner most thoughts about his lost love. But he felt that there was no one to serve as his confessor, no one into whose care he would discharge his burning secret. Some final degree of emotional release came only in his 80s as he poured out his soul in writing his autobiography, *Out of the Depths*. He had not talked about her to his friends and colleagues for all those years.

Why did Boisen continue to try to persuade Alice to marry him when she made it very clear that she was not interested? Why didn't he find another woman who would marry him? Why did he torture himself with the unrequited love of Alice? Why did she continue to see him after she had told him there was no future for them together in marriage?

One explanation might be that it is possible that most of his problem with Alice Batchelder was that it was too dangerous for him to be close to one person. She came out of the mists of legend and myth. She was his Beatrice, his muse, "the guiding hand," and I believe he did not desire to forfeit that blessing even though it meant he never married and fulfilled another desire, to have a family and carry on the Boisen name. In his "Epilogue" to the book *Out of the Depths*, he holds the same "love and honor" for Alice at 82 as he had at 25when he first met her on the campus of Indiana University.[132]

Fr. Henri J. M. Nouwen who wrote a doctoral dissertation on Boisen[133] saw Alice as a therapist. Nouwen wrote, "She is the curing authority to which the patient [Boisen] becomes more and more attached but who is also able to make him more and more aware of his attachment in such a way that he is slowly able to develop a more independent, mature relationship. The more we consider Boisen's autobiography, the more it becomes clear that this is the way in which Alice is seen. She constantly warns him when he goes too far and violates the contract, which is repeatedly phrased in terms as 'she gave her consent' or 'as it might be of help to me.'"[134]

Also, she is interwoven with his religious faith. In the end, she helped Boisen rid himself of the feeling of alienation and isolation and brought about a transformation that improved the religious values of his life. After a very long and painful relationship of dependency, Boisen was able to stop seeing Alice for his own needs. Even as early as 1921, he saw the love relationship as an "inner struggle and what might accurately be called the need for salvation."[135] When Alice died, Boisen was able to find his own grounding and give more than take. This resulted in his development of professional contextuality with many people in academia.

In Boisen's "Epilogue" to *Out of the Depths* he refers to "The Guiding Hand" he wrote about Alice and gave thanks to her, but I believe he really meant God. He made reference to Joseph and his brothers in the Hebrew Scriptures. When he wrote of the role Alice played in his life, he quoted from Joseph's words to his brothers when reconciliation had taken place, "Be not angry with yourselves because you sold me hither. So now, it was not you that sent me hither but God." I believe Boisen was saying in his 82nd year, it was really not Alice; it was God who was a "guiding hand" as well as an elusive figure in the care of his soul. He wrote: "I would be a man of little faith, if I did not recognize in this story the guiding hand of Intelligence beyond our own."[136]

Alice remains a mystery to us. There is little that leads us to her family of origin, to her work-a-day position in Chicago or earlier with the YWCA. Her death and the death of the relationship once and for all was the beginning of his creativity and his renewed vocation. He now had his own independent part to play in the world.

10

DARKNESS AND THE LITTLE KNOWN COUNTRY

Courtesy: Wylie House Museum, Indiana University
Anton Boisen in his mid-forties
Just prior to his first hospitalization

To catch up on the story of Boisen's life journey, we return to the year 1920. Upon his return from North Dakota in early October of that year, he went to live temporarily with his sister, brother-in-law, and mother in Massachusetts; he was still trying to find his professional identity. His former pastor in Bloomington, Rev. George Luccock, Chairperson of the Committee on Vacancies of the General Assembly of the Presbyterian Church, was willing to help him.

ANTON THEOPHILUS BOISEN:

Into the Depths of the Little Known Country

On October 6, 1920, in the process of writing a *Statement of Faith* in preparation for a call through the Presbyterian Church, Boisen became obsessed with delusional fantasies. He said: "A dramatic and severe disturbance plunged me as a patient into the insane asylum, with Dante's words: '"Abandon hope, all ye who enter here' swirling like a dense fog in my mind."[137] He descended into what he called "the little known country" of mental illness. In *Exploration of the Inner World, A Study of Mental Illness and Religious Experience*(1936) he wrote: "The experience at the psychopathic seemed to be that of passing through all the stages of individual development from the single cell onward. It was violent. There was no possibility of failing to recognize it for what it actually was – a psychosis of the most severity. At the same time I seemed to be passing through all the stages in the evolution of the race. I was carried back to the period of the deluge, back to the age of marshes and croaking frogs, back to the age of insects and also to an age of birds. I also visited the sun and moon and I even roamed all around the universe. My conscious self was indeed down in the lower regions at the mercy of all the strange and terrifying phantasms which were to me reality. It was a terrific life and death struggle in which all accepted belief and values were overturned, and I did not know what to believe. I was sure of just one thing, that things were not what they seemed. Many of the ideas that came to me were shocking, horrifying in the extreme; but even so, I can say there was no giving way to the lower tendencies."[138]

His diagnosis was Catatonic Schizophrenia.[139] At a later time, when he was hospitalized in Baltimore in 1935, he admitted that his initial breakdown had been related to Alice. The source of this break down was most certainly that he had failed to persuade Alice Batchelder to marry him. After nine years of rootlessness, he hoped that he would become re-established with her. It was not to be.

He was committed to Boston Psychopathic Hospital and later to Westboro State Hospital. He described his experience as "a most profound and unmistakable madness." In chapter four, "A Little Known Country" in his autobiography *Out of the Depths*, Boisen further describes his psychiatric delusions. "Everything began to whirl! It seemed the world was coming to an end…Some sort of change was due. Only a few tiny atoms we call 'men' were to be saved. I was to be one of these. I might, however, be of help to others." As the days went tediously on, he became violent, singing and shouting and pounding on the glass. He talked of wanting to die that he might be born again, repeatedly he rammed his head against a brick wall. This was a time of intense delusional ideation. "It seemed that the world was all ears and the words which I spoke would bring about my undoing," he "succeeded in climbing into the sun and was preoccupied with the moon. On the moon, all participants were obsessed with sex and reproduction. One's sex might change when one climbed onto the moon. Physicians would try to determine whether the individual was a man or a woman." He discovered he was neither. He believed that sacrifice meant he was "becoming a woman." He thought he was the woman, Mary Magdalene, and that he had "to go insane in order to get married." He thought he was of the lowest manner of being, and he often was found naked on the floor. Because he was always making plans to defeat his enemies he required continual "watchfulness." Doctors could not be trusted. Everything had a deeper meaning, the doctors, the attendants, what he ate, and what he did not eat. Once he believed that a little lamb was being born upstairs; and at the very same time, a horrible disaster was about to occur in which Christian civilization was to be destroyed. In a sort-of manic rite, he took his Bible, read at random as he had done many years ago. At that earlier time, his eyes fell on the passage, "Ask and you shall receive, seek and you shall find, knock and it shall be opened unto you." Looking back, almost forty years, that passage was something more than a coincidence. It was a synchronistic moment for Boisen.

In his *Statement of Belief* he was preparing, he wrote, "I believe that God was perfectly revealed in the life and teachings of Jesus of Nazareth. His patience with our shortcomings, his compassion upon our infirmities, his unfaltering faith in men, even his enemies, and his method of dealing with them, not through force, but through the power of love, culminating in his death upon the cross, where he died, the just for the unjust, the perfect for the imperfect, the strong for the weak."

Professor Glenn Asquith, Jr. described this experience of Boisen: "He began to have delusions about a Family of Four showing the strong, the weak, the perfect, and the imperfect. He diagramed the Family of Four and related it to his frustration over his desire to marry Alice. Essentially the scheme was telling Boisen that, because his love for Alice was based on his need for salvation, he was weak and imperfect. He therefore must give way to someone whose love was not based on need in order that more thoroughbred type of character may be produced."[140]

This was the first reference to the Family of Four. Boisen felt that the message in his hallucinations demanded that he give up the hope that had dominated his life for seventeen years, ever since he met Alice. He felt that his world was coming to an end.[141] The feelings for Alice Batchelder figured convincingly in his mental breakdown and also in the idea of the Family of Four. The Family of Four tended to figure in much of his fantasy world during all of his hospitalizations. The dominant idea was that the Family of

Four represented the fact that the Strong are to take care of the Weak, and the Perfect are to take care of the Imperfect. He felt that the weak and imperfect should no longer accept this sacrifice and that "they should be willing to give their lives, the imperfect for the perfect and the weak for the strong, that the divine may be freed from its prison house of infirmity and be able to come into the world in beauty and power." Boisen continued, "I believe that the family should consist of four and not of two, of the strong and perfect and of the guardian angels who in the joy of serving and sharing in the happiness of those they love will find compensation for the sacrifices that some will always have to make."

In the Family of Four, he alluded to the death of Jesus on the cross, "where he died: The Perfect for the Imperfect, the Strong for the Weak."

> The process has been going on for nineteen centuries. The strong have been giving themselves for the weak and the perfect for the imperfect. I believe the weak and the imperfect should no longer accept this sacrifice and that they should be willing to give their lives, the imperfect for the perfect and the weak for the strong, that the Divine may be freed from its prison house of infirmity and be able to come into the world in beauty and in power and not in disguise, and that the reign of love may be able to replace that of brute force and ruthless competition, where survival goes to the strong and to the merciless.[142]

He envisioned these types of people, the perfect, the imperfect, the strong, and the weak, as a forever intertwined, unified "Family of Four." During later hospitalizations, the "Family of Four," on one level, included both Helen Flanders Dunbar, who was for a while Director of the Council for the Clinical Training of Theological Students,[143] and The Reverend Dr. Austin Philip Guiles, the first Field Secretary of the CCTTS. Boisen interpreted the delusions, on one level, as instructing him to give Dunbar over to Guiles. Boisen believed that it was his task to keep the New York and the Boston groups together, eventually they grew further and further apart. The idea of the Family of Four will provide religious solutions to the problems left to humankind.

In his own words he wrote in *Out of the Depths*:

I was told that witches were around and from the ventilator shaft I picked up paper black cats and broom-sticks, and poke bonnets. I was greatly exercised and stuffed my blanket into the ventilator shaft. I finally not only worked out a way of checking the invasion of the black cats, but I found some sort of process of regeneration that could be used to save other people. I had, it seemed, broken an opening in the wall which separated medicine and religion. I was told to feel on the back of my neck and I would find here a sign of my new mission.[144]

In the midst of these bizarre delusions, Boisen received a revelation that had to do with *"breaking down the wall between religion and medicine."* To this task, Boisen dedicated the rest of his life. He found meaning and purpose in the midst of the terrifying delusion. It was his way of salvation, "out of the depths." He wrote later that at the time of his first hospitalization he had been absorbed in prayer, and he felt that he had never been closer to the things of central importance than he had at that time.[145]

All that had gone before entered into this experience. His long educational history, the memory of his father and his mother's influence, the many influences of life with grandfather Theophilus Adam Wylie and his mentor at Indiana University, Dr. William Lowe Bryan, teachers and friends, and the varying experiences in forestry, theological education at Union Seminary, church survey, and the congregational pastorates had molded the Anton Boisen that entered into this crucial experience. The outcome of the experience was a source of new ideas, new insights, and a new trust in his intuition. Actually his acute stage of schizophrenia lasted approximately two weeks, but he continued to stay in the hospital for thirteen months.

During those two weeks his experience was wild, and to a degree destructive, yet it brought him closer to a solution of his vocation. It showed him a vast "unexplored territory and an unmet need of greatest importance." He wrote, "Here I saw my future work."[146]

In the opening lines of the "Introduction" to *The Exploration of the Inner World*, Boisen wrote, "To be plunged as a patient into a hospital for the insane may be a tragedy or it may be an opportunity. For me, it has been an opportunity. It has introduced me to a new world of absorbing interest and profound significance; it has shown me that world throughout its entire range, from the bottom most depths of the nether regions to the heights of religious experience at its best; it has made me aware of relationships between two important fields of human experience that thus far have been held strictly apart; and it has given me a task in which I find the meaning and purpose of my life."[147]

He believed that there was an important relationship between acute psychotic episodes and resultant religious experiences. This became apparent to him when he was confined to Westboro State Mental Hospital. He felt that certain types of mental disorders and certain types of religious experiences were alike attempts at reorganization. He associated crisis with religious "quickening." They are moments bringing forth change either for the better or for the worse. For him to suggest that he believed that the experience of his mental illness had some purpose, and to persist in the idea that insanity is one of the nation's most pressing problems, and that it was his task to investigate it, or to suggest that there was a connection between the experience of mental illness and the religious was unheard of at this time in medical and religious history.

There had been, in the distant past, a time when religion and medicine was more holistic. Religion and medicine talked and walked the same path for the good of the suffering one. That had faded into the background by the latter part of the nineteenth century. Professor Edward Larson, in *Summer for the Gods, The Scopes Trial and America's Continuing Debate over Science and Religion* (1997), wrote that by the turn of the 20th century secular historians and essayists rather than theologians were largely responsible for keeping alive the public perception of enmity between religion and science.[148] Anton Boisen's view of "breaking down the wall..." was prudent and prophetic for the time.

He went so far as to say that in his judgment the religious situation was the only true and lasting solution of the difficult personal problems with which we deal in mental disorders. He felt that if he had not had the resources of his religious belief and religious inspiration he would have been "crushed never to rise again." It was his hope to give the rest of his life to the problem society faces with the mentally ill.

It needs to be said, also, that he believed that there was mental illness that was not religious phenomena and the challenge was, and still is, to know the difference. He was aware that some of his psychotic experience was non productive; however, he did not develop that Shadow side of his personhood as fully as he did those experiences that he felt had religious import

He was satisfied that the course was clear for him. He felt that religious interpretations of the past experience of his mental illness, the belief that there was some purpose in it, defined his mission. These thoughts were a refuge and strength to him and prepared him for the task. His experience of hospitalization was a religious conversion, a personal encounter with the Holy in which he found healing for his soul. He emerged stronger and convinced that the religious solutions was the only true and lasting solution of the difficult personal problems with which we deal in mental illness.

In a lecture that Boisen gave at a Conference of the Council for the Clinical Training of Theological Students at Worcester State Hospital on August 23, 1930, he commented on his religious conversion and way of salvation:

"As I look back upon the events leading up to my entry into this territory, I recall in particular two remarks. On the evening before I was sent to the hospital (1920), I informed my family that I had come to the conclusion that the most important problem before the world today was that of insanity and that I had decided to investigate it. And then two days later in the Psychopathic Hospital, I informed one of the doctors that I had broken through the wall between religion and medicine. Now these were just crazy ideas. Where they came from, I do not know. It had not occurred to me to consider myself insane. I was too busy settling the affairs of the universe for that. To this general program, I had previously given no thought and yet now, at the end of ten years, I am much of the same opinion still. In the territory opened up by this experience of mental disorder, I see an unexplored country of untold significance to those who would understand the nature and function of religion and the laws for the care of the soul. And in this undertaking of ours, I see precisely an attempt to bring together two hitherto separate fields of experience and effort and to promote an understanding between the clerical and medical professions in regard to a problem which belongs to one just as much as it does to the other. I am of course making an assumption that will be challenged by some psychiatrists; I am assuming that most of the disorders with whom we are dealing at this hospital are in the strict sense of the term spiritual problems. They are experiences rather than diseases. They are to be explained as reactions to life situations, rather than in terms of organic pathology. They have to do with philosophy of life, rather than with what can be examined in the test tube or under the microscope. Organic involvements there are indeed, and these must never be left out of account; but these I look upon as secondary rather than primary."[149]

During his long hospitalization, he began reading Freud, corresponding with friends and studying fellow patients. The letters he wrote at this time go into detail and are extremely well written, thought through, and documented about his time in the hospital. Fred Eastman brought Freud to Boisen's attention. Henri Nouwen wrote about Boisen that "the main role of Freud was to articulate ideas and concepts that were already present in Boisen's mind." Boisen wrote that "the interpretation I had arrived at before I ever heard of Freud."[150]

He felt glad to have the support of such a famous person as Dr. Sigmund Freud. Boisen was especially attracted to Freud's belief that abnormal or insane conditions have a purpose. They are deep-seated conflicts between great subconscious forces, and the cure is to be found, not in suppression of the symptoms, but in the resolution of the conflict. Boisen wrote, "Freud holds that in practically every case of successful treatment in which the sex instinct is involved, the patient's affections are transferred to the physician. This must be wisely utilized as fundamental to the process of cure, namely, the elimination of the transference as soon as the right time comes. This marks the completion of the process of cure."[151] Boisen sees his own case as precisely what has been happening to him. And

Alice Batchelder is his physician.

It was through his letters to Norman Nash, a friend from Union now teaching at the Episcopal Theological School in Cambridge, that Boisen was introduced to The Reverend Dr. Elwood Worcester, a prominent clergy and psychologist. After corresponding, they met for their first counseling session on November 15, 1921. Eventually, with Dr. Elwood Worcester's help, Boisen obtained a conditional release from Westboro in late January 1922.

Boisen emerged from the experience of his hospitalization with a new sense of what he was meant to be and do. He had gained poise, serenity, and a more organized resolve as a result of his breakdown and recovery. He had now found his vocation and was finally free to be innovative. In the midst, Boisen found himself, acknowledged the value of events in the past, and saw clearly into the future. Writing in *The Exploration of the Inner World* he said that "back of this solution of my problem, there was something more than just myself, something not just blindly purposive but a guiding intelligence. The real danger was, I think, that of forgetting and of failing to heed the vision that comes to us at those times when we stand face to face with the ultimate realities of our lives. It would be indeed a tragedy in my own case if the idea of God did not remain for me something very much more than just a symbol."[152]

Mystical Encounter with God

Boisen claimed a direct mystical encounter with God in the midst of his mental illness during 1920-21. He came to call this his "guiding intelligence." He brought out of this experience something new, something that he did not take into it, and this was because he had encountered God in a way he had never encountered God before. It is similar to the experience, in scripture, of Jacob in his journey to meet his brother Esau, when he wrestled with the Holy in the Jabbok valley and came out with a new vision for life, now as a wounded healer.

Focusing his attention on the relationship between religious experience and mental illness, his own experience became the model. He wrote, "Certain types of mental disorder are *not in themselves evil,* but they are problem solving experiences. They are attempts at reorganization in which the entire personality, to its bottommost depths, is aroused and its forces marshaled to meet the danger of personal failure and isolation. According to this hypothesis the primary evil in functional disorder lies in the realm of personal relationship, particularly to that which is for most represented in the idea of God." [153]

This dramatic insight into his mental illness, its relation to religious experience, and the idea of God, had been first encountered in Dr. William Lowe Bryan's philosophy and psychology class at Indiana University. Dr Bryan's "Plateaus in Learning" taught that at the peak of a human crisis there is often a turning toward healing, toward reorganization, toward reconnection. From the arrhythmia of despair, there emerged a new rhythm, the vital primal rhythm of life that Dr. Bryan called a "religious experience of the Holy." This theory remained a central foundation to Boisen's theology, and his understanding of mental illness throughout the remainder of his life.

His mental illness was not so much a break-down as it was a break-through. For Boisen, mental illness was a way some deal with an intolerable sense of personal failure and guilt.

James Hillman, a Jungian therapist and educator, in a lecture he gave in 1985 at the Eranos Center in Ascona, Switzerland, used Anton Boisen as one of three case studies for his lecture titled *On Paranoia.* He made this statement about Boisen's claim that God is not driven off with the disease, if we are faithful to the delusion itself. Hillman said, "Recovery means recovering the divine from within the disorder, seeing that its contents are authentically religious. These delusions may be psychogenic; nonetheless, they are theogenic, originating with God. We may attribute them not only to the unseen psychodynamics of the human mind, but also to the dynamics of the unseen order itself. The psychopathic ward is also a place of epiphany, the disciplines endured there are of the spirit, and the enclosure a theology school. For Boisen, the hospital is a place to learn about the hidden God by means of delusions."[154] This is precisely what Boisen believed and regarding which he was about to be engaged.

Dr. Lucy Bregman, Professor of Religion at Temple University, wrote an article for the *Journal of Religion and Health* entitled "Anton Boisen Revisited." She pointed out "that in the chapter on 'George Fox among the Doctors' in Boisen's *The Exploration of the Inner World*, Jung's therapy and theory of psychosis receive the most favorable treatment of any of the many options discussed in this chapter. Jung, according to Boisen, appreciated the positive function of religion in personal integration, the meaningfulness of the psychotic experience, and the collective nature of symbolism."[155]

Boisen wrote about the break up between Freud and Jung. It came because of Jung's resolve that in the unconscious there is something else besides pleasure-seeking, something purposive and forward looking that expresses itself in the encounter with the Holy.

Jung was critical of Freud's conception of sex as the basic human drive. He thought of sex as one aspect of a general drive or psychic energy. Life for Jung is essentially purposive. Jung expresses frankly his interest in religions. The concept of God is a necessary psychological function of humankind's irrational nature. In Jung's personality theory, the question of God's existence is beside the point. Everywhere and in all times men and women have developed, spontaneously, religious forms and expressions and the human psyche from all time has been shot through with religious feelings and ideas.[156]

Six months after Boisen was discharged from Westboro State Hospital, he wrote an interpretation of his experience that he titled "Studies of a Little Known Country." In the first paragraph he set forth an idea that became his own "shaping vision" the remainder of his life He wrote:

A fifteen month sojourn in a hospital for the insane may be a tragedy or it may be an opportunity, all depends upon what it does to you or what you do to it. Which it is to prove in my own case is as yet too early to tell but I prefer to take the favorable interpretation. In any case it gave me the opportunity to study from the inside a very *little known country* whose significance for the great problems of human personality seems to me far greater than generally recognized. [157]

The document that was begun in the summer month of June 1921, and was completed in August of 1922, was a well thought out, comprehensive call for the church in America to wake up to the need for pastors and chaplains to be involved in the care of souls in mental health institutions. His concern was that the church had stayed away from providing soul-care to those in mental hospitals. He acknowledges the difficulty for the church to involve itself in such a ministry, but he said in so many words – do it anyway. It was hard for Jesus and it was difficult for Paul, but they did it anyway. He felt that the obvious thing to do would be to establish chaplaincies at some of the institutions for the insane. "Such chaplaincies could be under the auspices of the Federal Council of Churches. Also, the chaplains must be trained. No one should undertake a task of this nature without familiarizing himself or herself with the present knowledge in regard to the human personality both in health and in disease and of the approved method of treatment."[158]

For Boisen, there was fore-warning, then the experience(s) of catastrophe, a prospect of regeneration, and recovery as a "new being," phenomena that he experienced as authentic religious focus. Yet, sometimes he was deluded because some of the ideas he continued to have were utterly alien to anything of which he had ever heard. What of the Hebrew prophets. For example, Hosea is a case in point. Hosea was commanded by God to marry the prostitute Gomer as a sign to depict God's relationship to Israel. Boisen's value was precisely in the spontaneous novelty of experimental learning. This is precisely what mission and prophecy demand. Boisen now had a mission and he became a prophet, and the novelty was that his message had to do with experience; it had to do with the empirical method of learning theology. Does not his supreme value lie precisely in the novelty of the empirical (pragmatic) method of doing theology?

By November 1922, he began working for The Reverend Dr. Elwood Worcester, doing casework for the Emmanuel Church's Department of Community Service. Also at this time, Boisen participated in Dr. Richard Cabot's case seminar in Social Ethics at Harvard University. His first case concerned "Albert A," one of the fellow patients he had studied while at Westboro State Hospital.

Boisen applied, and was accepted, to work in the Social Service Department at Boston Psychopathic Hospital; while there he prepared more than 40 case histories for Cabot's class. He took residence at the Episcopal Theological School where he attended classes. He also studied at Andover Theological School as a special student and at Harvard Graduate School of Arts and Studies in the Division of Psychology and Social Ethics. In 1923 he received an

AM degree from Harvard.

In 1923, as a student at Harvard University, he wrote a paper entitled, "To Give the Rest of my Life to the Problem." In this paper, he wrote, "During my stay at Westboro Hospital, I once remarked to one of the physicians that while I knew that most of my ideas had been absurd and grotesque and many of them most shocking, I still believed that the experience had some meaning and that there was some purpose to it. The physician replied that I must get rid of such an idea entirely. Shortly after that, an invitation from one of my friends to spend Christmas with him was refused on the ground that he still believes that he has had no serious illness and that there has been a plan in the experience through which he has passed, I have observed in other cases that any suggestion that a patient has a sense of 'mission' is regarded by psychiatrists as a very unfavorable symptom." His delusions and the meanings derived from them represented the task to which he would now dedicate his life.

Courtesy: Indiana University
Dr. William Lowe Bryan, Ph.D.
Lecturer of Philosophy and Psychology

DARKNESS AND THE LITTLE KNOWN COUNTRY

Dr. William Lowe Bryan has already been introduced several times. He was a major influence throughout Boisen's life. He was from Monroe County, Indiana, the son of a Presbyterian minister and Eliza Phillips Bryan. He graduated from Indiana University in 1884 with a degree in the Ancient Classics, and received a Master's degree in Philosophy at Indiana University He was invited to join the faculty of the Greek Department, and in 1885 he was appointed Associate Professor of Philosophy. However, his interest shifted to psychology, and he went to Germany to study at the University of Berlin. When he retuned he was named full professor and granted money to conduct research in human reaction times. He opened a psychological laboratory at Indiana University in 1888, the second such laboratory in the history of the USA. The first being at the University of Cornell established in 1881.[159] He decided to study under Dr. G. Stanley Hall at Clark University and received a Ph.D. in psychology in 1892. Dr. Bryan was a leader in the early study of psychology in America. Upon return from the study with Dr. G. Stanley Hall, he was appointed Vice President of the University; and in 1902 he was elected President of Indiana University and oversaw the development of the institution for 35 years.

Although Bryan was not an ordained minister, in 1906 he preached what he called "a sermon" as the address to the graduating class at Indiana University. "My Children," he said, "believe this Man. With Jesus you will find a place within, where there are neither curses nor despair, nor wars, but where there lives an unconquerable courage for every circumstance and for every task which can come to you before the going down of the sun."

A pastoral letter to Boisen from Bryan, now President Emeritus of Indiana University, serves as an example of their relationship. He was writing to Boisen in 1941.[160] It seemed that it was prompted after Boisen had had difficulty with a Bible class in Olney, Illinois.

He had written Bryan about it. Bryan wrote back, "Dear Anton, Your experience at the Bible Class in Olney brings to my mind the practice of the Apostle Paul in adjusting his message to his audiences. This, as you know, is well illustrated in the Acts and is stated by him plainly, even bluntly, to the Corinthians. He had a profound metaphysic and theology, but he said to the Corinthians you cannot understand the hidden wisdom...I therefore preach to you nothing but Christ and Christ crucified..." He goes on in the letter to state the order of salvation, from his point of view, citing Dr. Albert Schweitzer who said that Paul had three conceptions of salvation that did not quarrel with one another. He goes on in the letter to cite Paul's metaphysic as coming from the Hebrew philosophers and from the Greeks: Plato, Philo, Aristotle, and Plotinus. Paul's way to salvation is not mechanical, not legal, but is based on the belief that we are bound together in one bundle of life with each other and with the Christ. He ends the pastoral letter to Boisen saying, "This is a long letter. What I have in mind is that a minister does well indeed if he can follow Paul's example, talking to children that they can understand him, talking to businessmen in a giant Bible class so that they can understand him, but always with the underlying spirit of the Christ that radiates through whatever he says." He encouraged Boisen to "make it simple" as a minister. He ends the letter, "Affectionately, William Lowe Bryan." [161]

On the side of the religious, this letter from Bryan is an example of the dynamics of their relationship, and the respect they had one for the other. Bryan's admonition in general and specific terms, regarding what a minister needs to be attentive to, was wisdom for the ministers and for Boisen. It is a letter representing Bryan's faith in the Bible and in particular the Apostle Paul's message. Also, theologically, Bryan's statement "we are bound together in one bundle of life with each other and with the Christ" has a similar point in Boisen's theology of Redemption being through the "fellowship of best." Boisen said that all true life is social life, is life-together. In the language of Martin Heidegger it is 'being- with" and "being-for" the other. He goes into greater depth, in particular the social dynamic of religious life, in *Religion in Crisis and Custom: A Sociological and Psychological Study of Religion* with special reference to American Protestantism.[162] Bryan influenced Boisen's respect for traditional religious thought through their friendship

Courtesy: ACPE Office, Decatur, GA
Richard Cabot, MD, Medical Reformer

Dr. Richard Cabot, also, made an impact on Boisen's life. Dr Cabot was a well known medical reformer during this era. He was on the faculty of Harvard University, and was one of America's best known physicians. Cabot taught by presenting case histories to his students and then asking for a diagnosis and treatment for the patients. These clinical procedures became the Clinical Pathologic

Conference, still used as a standard teaching method in medicine. This became a framework for Anton Boisen's case study method. Cabot wrote and spoke extensively on medical ethics. His primary concerns were clinical and humanistic. In 1920, Cabot left full-time medical work to teach social ethics at Andover Theological Seminary in Newton Centre, Massachusetts, and the Episcopal Theological Seminary in Cambridge, Massachusetts.

In 1905, Cabot founded hospital social work at Massachusetts General Hospital and twenty years later he confronted theological students with his appeal for the introduction of a clinical year in theological education. In 1922, he proposed that seminary students have a year of supervised experience with people suffering from the "infirmities of humankind" just as medical students do before going to their work as licensed physicians. Dr. Cabot MD wanted theology brought into the situation of human suffering. He encouraged theological educators to provide competence in pastoral work and training in pastoral theology. Cabot was a recognized pioneer in efforts to define the physician's role in human well-being and in his work at seminaries.

A few months after Boisen began a summer program at Worcester, Dr. Cabot's "Plea for a Clinical Year in the Course of Theological Study" was written. It had a major impact on the founding of the clinical pastoral education movement. Cabot felt that as medical students learn medicine through practice and observation so could theological students benefit from a similar kind of clinical experience before they go out to congregations and specialized ministries. He urged theological students to get experience in ministry outside of the classroom. He wanted students to use theology with troubled individuals. He felt the year of internship ought to be a year of applied theology "in the practice of gospel Christianity," and not training in secular science.[163]

DARKNESS AND THE LITTLE KNOWN COUNTRY

After Boisen's hospitalization in 1930, Cabot did not trust Boisen's judgment and leadership any more. Cabot would in fact have little to do with Boisen who believed that mental illness was due to inner psychological pathology. As far back as 1928, Cabot had told both Anton Boisen and Austin Philip Guiles that he did not accept the psychogenic theory of mental illness. Cabot was a firm believer in the organic foundation of mental illness. He leaned more toward the biological. Despite the fact that Cabot had rejected Boisen's view of mental illness and had lost confidence in his ability to function as a supervisor, Boisen publicly, and graciously, paid tribute to Cabot's impact on his early career. The most significant impact being Boisen's reading the book *Differential Diagnosis* where Cabot discusses his case method.

Dr. Brian W. Grant, Professor of Christian Ministries at Christian Theological Seminary in Indianapolis, wrote in his *Schizophrenia: A Source of Social Insight* (1975) about the idea that schizophrenia can be a source of social insight. Schizophrenia is the disorder that has as its basis the interplay between a family and the broader society of which he/she is a part. Schizophrenia can provide a prophetic insight, and Grant believes that the person's suffering can point to insight concerning a particular social and familial stress that produced the illness. The schizophrenic can view the world in different ways, apart from stereotypes and tradition; can speak the truth with power much better than those bound by tradition. Bryan Grant relies on the life and works of Anton Boisen to support his thesis.[164] I was informed recently that in Chinese, the symbol for "crisis" is made of the two words "Tragedy" or "Opportunity." So it was with Anton Theophilus Boisen, he turned what might have been tragedy into a grand opportunity.

11

MYSTERY OF LIGHT RESTORATION TO A NEW VISION

Boisen kept a diary for much of his professional life. He seldom wrote anything about his life outside the ministry; however it is full of experiences, thoughts and conclusions professionally. In his diary of 1924, on March 12, he records, "Dr. Bryan of Worcester State Hospital has agreed to the plan of a chaplain, and I am to see him Monday for an interview." On March 19, he wrote. "Went to Worcester in the morning. I had a very satisfactory talk with Dr. Bryan. He was very interested in the material I gave him." Then on March 21, he wrote: "I saw Dr. Bryan this afternoon. He seemed much interested in the Chaplaincy proposition. I am to see him again next week." On April 21 Boisen got a letter from Dr. Bryan. Dr. Bryan said "the budget will not permit of my being hired before October 1." However, he was hired by July 13, when he records in his diary that he was settling in his office.[165]

July 1, 1924, Dr. William A. Bryan, Superintendent of the Worcester State Hospital in Massachusetts (Superintendent 1921-

1940), with the support of the Massachusetts Congregational Conference, and the Chicago Theological Seminary, appointed The Reverend Anton T. Boisen as chaplain for the hospital.[166] Clinical pastoral education is indebted to Dr. Bryan for the risk he took in hiring Boisen. The well known comment that Dr. Bryan made when asked about hiring a chaplain full time. "Why, I would hire a horse doctor if he could help my patients."[167]

On Christmas break, 1924, two "young gentlemen" from Dr. Cabot's class at Episcopal Theological Seminary, Perry Smith and Charles Graves, came to see Boisen to ask him about summer employment as attendants at Worcester State. The students were in the class that inspired Dr. Cabot's "Plea for a Clinical Year in the Course of Theological Study," printed in *Survey Graphic* for September 1925. [168] Even before that date, Boisen pointed out in a letter to Fred Kuether saying that Dr. Cabot's first public lecture or paper on the subject of seminary students doing work in a hospital was published in the *Christian Register* about January 1924 under the title of 'The Cure of Souls."[169]

Neither student from Cabot's class came to Worcester during the next summer of 1925, but they had given Boisen an idea. He made plans for a clinical training program for that same summer. He went to Boston, then to New York, to see whether there were not some theological students who might be interested in a summer program at Worcester. During that summer four theological students came to Worcester, two to work on the wards and to serve in other ways, one to be his assistant, and one student to work with the Social Service Department. During that summer, of the four theological students who came to Worcester State Hospital, two stayed to the end of the unit. One of the participants was Helen Flanders Dunbar, a student from Union Seminary in New York. She stayed only about a month.[170] Participants, along with Dunbar, were Melvin Bowmar from Boston University School of Religious Education, Carl Romig Hutchinson from Chicago Theological Seminary, and Tom Lawton from Harvard Divinity School.[171] All went well, except for one of the students assigned to an admission ward. He was frightened by a patient who brandished a table fork, and the student fled to a closet locking the door. Boisen notes that it took a long time to live that down.

The students were assigned as Attendants on a hospital ward, went to the lectures by medical staff, and didactics on pastoral theology by Boisen or a guest he might involve from a nearby seminary. There was always the case of "Albert W," or "Oscar O," or "The Page of the Blessed Virgin." Boisen selected from a large volume of cases he had collected to demonstrate his theory of mental illness. They led in worship, studied Boisen's case studies, and wrote their own case study of a patient.[172] Boisen's genius was the belief that abnormal psychology could throw light on religious experiences was an innovation that he taught students who entered the clinical education program.

Boisen's first training program was designed to research theological issues through work with what he called "living human documents." Although the initial program was very modest, having ended with only two students completing the program, Boisen was encouraged to try it again the following year in 1926. Then the program began to expand. Subsequent years showed a steady increase in clinical training being offered to seminary students and clergy not only at Worcester, but at other centers in the New England and Mid Atlantic states. Individuals like Donald Beatty, Carroll Wise, and Austin Philip Guiles were willing to give themselves to the world of clinical pastoral education to eventually become faculty as Supervisors themselves. Boisen wrote in "Theological Education via the Clinic," *Religious Education*, (March 1930) "of all the work done by our students, the most important both for the standpoint of the hospital and of the students themselves is undoubtedly the work on the wards." Not only did the program expand in mental health settings; but it also, by 1937, spread to the general hospitals and correctional institution settings.

Worcester State Hospital

Courtesy: the Author 2008
Kirkbride Hall, built in 1870

When Boisen was first hired by Worcester State Hospital, he was to be solely a chaplain to patients, families, and staff. He would provide counseling, conduct worship services, and educational possibilities, but he would not be in charge of recreational activities. Boisen wanted an activity for students so that they would be recognized immediately by the hospital community. Therefore, he initiated a recreational program that was utilized for that purpose.

Other colleagues in the pastoral care movement criticized Boisen for not sticking exclusively to chaplaincy, but he felt it was a wholesome thing for the students to come in as "friends" to the patients by taking part in recreational activities, and not merely conducting conventional religious activity. He had done this in the rural parishes where he ministered, building bridges for relationships by becoming involved himself, and involving the congregation in social service functions with the community. Boisen brought them into contact with many groups as students formed relationships with patients and hospital personnel. The students would deliver the hospital newsletter, for example, from unit to unit throughout the hospital and thereby come to know the units and the staff. Also, in collecting the news for the newsletter, the students would come in contact with many people.

Courtesy Hammond Library Boisen collection CTS
Boisen's Second Group of theological students at Worcester State Hospital 1926
Front row: Johnson (Garrett), Anton Boisen, Allen (Boston University). Back row: Stuart (Boston University), Module (Harvard)

ANTON THEOPHILUS BOISEN:

During the summer of 1926, there were four students, seven in1927. In his diary he gives an account of the early work with students in Clinical Pastoral Training. He often had Dr. Lewis Hill, a psychiatrist on staff of the hospital, help in the group seminars. They did team teaching.

In his diary on July 16, 1927, he wrote about the decision of Donald Beatty, a Boston University student   He was trying to land him for the coming year.   Beatty seemed much pleased, and he talked as if he had decided to come. Boisen wrote: "Beatty informed me today that he was willing to stay here for a full year." Boisen was much delighted at this outcome. Beatty served as Boisen's assistant at Worcester for a few years. He then became the chaplain supervisor at Pittsburgh City Home and Hospitals. Later he transferred to Elgin State Hospital as chaplain supervisor and remained there until 1942. At the end of that summer he became an Army chaplain.[173]

Boisen also developed a course in Abnormal Psychology at Boston University School of Theology from 1928-1930. He was assisted in the course by Dr. Lewis Hill, Assistant Superintendent at Worcester State Hospital. Both Reverend Don Beatty, and Reverend Carroll Wise, helped Boisen in the course.[174]

From 1925 through 1930, thirty five theological students attended the program at Worcester State Hospital. Out of that number, twenty-one entered congregational ministry.   Others continued training and were serving in various specialized ministry settings. Eight went on to graduate study to prepare to be teachers of pastoral ministry. The vast majority of theological students who were in the early training went into the pastorate, there to apply the learning in clinical pastoral education to ordinary problems of average congregational life. This energized him.

By 1930, training had greatly expanded. Dr. Cabot's call for a "clinical year" in his class at the Episcopal Theological Seminary was the spark, concurrent with Boisen's initial unit at Worcester that set off the clinical pastoral education movement.[175] It was the steady work of Anton Boisen at Worcester State Hospital that actually carried out training and established the model for those who followed. The students were challenged by Boisen's view that there are disorders of emotion and volition, of belief and attitude, rooted not in cerebral disease or breaking down of the reasoning processes, but which for the most part are examples of the age-old conflict that the Apostle Paul describes as the conflict between the law that is in our minds and that which is in our hearts and human desire.

In 1925, Anton Boisen wrote one of his first, of many, essays entitled, "In Defense of Mr. Bryan, A Personal Confession by a Disciple of Dr. Fosdick." This essay was occasioned by the most widely publicized misdemeanor case in American history, [176] the "Scopes Trial." John Thomas Scopes v. State of Tennessee, 1925.

First, he wrote about William Jennings Bryan and the very large and important group whose spokesman he was – the Protestant evangelical and fundamentalist groups. Second, he addressed Dr. Harry Emerson Fosdick (a well known liberal theologian) because of his open-minded attitude toward the conclusions of modern science and their attempt to interpret the old faith in terms of modern thought. Boisen wrote that Fosdick agreed that the Christian church must have an authoritative message, but he was not ready to go back to the traditional authority and the biblical literalism espoused by William Jennings Bryan. Then Boisen made this somewhat astonishing yet profoundly truthful observation: "I am inclined to believe that the weakness of the liberal group lies precisely in the fact that it has not yet gone *far enough*. Liberal theology has merely surrendered the authority of the tradition without freeing itself from the traditional point of view."[177] Boisen considered himself a "disciple of Fosdick," but when Fosdick read the manuscript, he wanted nothing to do with it. Fosdick said that Boisen could publish the article only over his dead body.[178] He did.

Boisen wrote further in this article, "People who have no message for the soul that is sick and who place their trust in religions education and programs of social reform, I hold with Mr. Bryan and his group that the central business of the church must ever be the saving of souls, and that it must speak with authority." The method, however, differed for Boisen. He preferred that there not be a return to the literal written record, "but a return to the experience of *existence* and then the foundation of *essence* central to Him who came to seek and to save the lost."[179]

The "In Defense of the Mr. Bryan" represented a thorough depiction of Boisen's early theological grounding - the *conservative Covenanter Presbyterian years* within the household of his Grandfather Theophilus Wylie. And, also, it represented *the progressive liberal theology* he embraced once he had developed his own unique spiritual formation at Union Seminary. It is a very good example of both aspects of Boisen's theology, at the beginning of his professional life as a chaplain and pastoral care educator.

On the Faculty at Chicago Theological Seminary

Beginning the fall of 1926, Boisen had an appointment to teach at Chicago Theological Seminary. At this Seminary the climate was right for a man like Boisen. Boisen was a friend of Reverend Arthur E. Holt. He met him when he was pastor in Wabaunsee, Kansas and Holt was in near-by Manhattan, Kansas. Boisen had learned sociological methods in research from Holt. When he had inaugurated a country church social action program, Boisen became very interested in his work.

Holt had recently been appointed head professor in the Department of Social Ethics at Chicago Theological Seminary. The seminary was a pioneer in new ventures and innovation from its very beginning. President Albert W. Palmer appointed Fred Eastman in Religious Literature and Drama, Arthur Cushman McGiffert, Jr. as Chair of Systematic Theology, and, on Arthur Holt's recommendation, Anton Boisen as Research Associate in the Social Ethics Department. Later Boisen became Professional Lecturer in Practical Theology. Arthur Holt wanted Boisen to spend the fall quarter on campus at Chicago Theological Seminary. He worked it out with the hospitals and with the help of students who were responsible for the ministry at Worcester and then Elgin the first semester of the academic year. With the help of Reverend Don Beatty, Boisen's assistant beginning in 1927, and Reverend Carroll Wise who, beginning in 1930, was in charge at Worcester, Boisen was free to teach at Chicago Theological Seminary each fall. Carroll Wise came as a student, and he stayed on, becoming Boisen's assistant and eventually his successor at Worcester. The move to Elgin made it possible for Boisen to be closer to Chicago Theological Seminary.

After a journey in supervision in Pittsburgh, Donald Beatty followed Boisen to Elgin and led the supervisory program when Boisen taught at CTS. These supervisors helped immensely in making it possible for Boisen to be free to teach at the seminary where he continued as a Research Associate in the Psychology of Religion Department. His tenure on the faculty at Chicago Theological Seminary was through 1942.

"He Never Learned To Talk About the Weather"

He did not know how to talk with people in general conversation.

Dr. Arthur Cushman McGiffert, Jr., in reminiscing about his relationship with Boisen, said: "He never learned to talk about the weather."

For example, the Reverend Lennart Cedarleaf, a student of Boisen's, invited him to his home for a visit; and he simply sat there for an hour or more absolutely silent. He liked to be in the midst of a social situation, but had little need to communicate. His affect was very flat most of the time. He seldom engaged in the give-and-take of personal interaction in his clinical pastoral education groups as well. The positive side of this was that he was a driven advocate of his method and his way of correlating self-understanding with basic theology.[180]

The negative side gave way to separation, loneliness, and a feeling of isolation. In listening to the audio tapes of the Historical Committee for the Association for Clinical Pastoral Education, and reading stories about Boisen by McGiffert, Cedarleaf, Oates, Wise, McPeek, and several others, my impression is that he apparently had learned how to disguise insecurities behind a mask of enigmatic silence.[181]

Boisen often wrote about his horrifying fear of being isolated. The characteristics of his affect at these times resembled a person who was bound with guilt and failure. The core issues were fear and insecurity resulting in isolation.

Lennart Cedarleaf, again, said of Boisen, "Anton was a benign, non-threatening human being. He was able, in a non-threatening way, to draw out life stories from the other very easily; this was especially true with patients who were going through what he went through in a mental hospital. His nonverbal communication was quite practiced and strong. I was impressed that he was totally interested in me and did not give me orders. He was interested in what I was doing as an approach to the religious. I was impressed with what he could educe from me."[182]

Another student, Anne Parrott, a graduate of Chicago Theological Seminary who became a clinical psychologist, said of Boisen. "He was like a man in a dark coat, a very isolated figure." His isolation was central to his life.

A student at Chicago Theological Seminary who lived on the same floor of the dormitory with him said: "He never talked to us, we never talked to him."[183] He had little sense of humor. Again, Dr. McGiffert said, "I cannot remember his face with a smile. He had a very narrow strip of experience." In the photographs of Boisen that I have seen, he seldom smiled as most people do when their picture is being taken. He did, however, become enthusiastic about his program; and he would get provoked when at informal settings someone would get off the subject. He was very intense.

The Reverend Clarence Bruninga, a student of Boisen, and a successor at Elgin State Hospital, said in a phone interview with the author, that when Boisen was with students he tended to be detached and distant. In class, he presented his own case material. The clinical report material was read and reviewed by Boisen's assistants. To compensate for his isolation and shyness, both at Worcester and at Elgin, he had an assistant who related with the students. He was a professional theological researcher. He did not relate well out of the clinical setting, neither in a clinical pastoral education group nor in the wider communities of life.

Psychologist Dr. Paul Pruyser at the Menninger Clinic in Topeka, Kansas said, "Boisen emphasized corporate worship at Elgin when Council supervisors were dealing with individuals." This seems to fit into the notion of being an isolated person. He wanted to have the reinforcement of others in this formal way, among his "Fellowship of the Best"; but he did not want to get close. Most of the problem with Alice Batchelder was that he could not become intimate. It was too dangerous to be close to one person. Dr. McGiffert said: "This did not ruin him; it just ruined it for being a friend. He was a creative person."[184]

The psychiatrist, Dr. Harry Stack Sullivan (1892-1949), had an influence on Boisen. During the early years the journal *Psychiatry* that Sullivan edited, Boisen was among the journal's most regular contributors. He wrote eight articles and four book reviews for *Psychiatry*. Most of them dealt with the psychosocial aspects of religious experience, derived from Boisen's interviews and empirical case histories. He had a long friendship with Sullivan who was interested in his religious ideas. Sullivan called his approach an interpersonal theory of psychiatry because he believed psychiatry is the study of what goes on between people. For Sullivan, relationships are primary. His interpersonal concepts had many parallel possibilities with biblical characters and themes. Love, ethical notions, covenant and the encounter with God were essential to Sullivan, and he was prone to use these symbols in his therapy.[185]

Boisen came to believe that his sense of guilt was essentially a social judgment that operated upon and within him. From childhood, he felt this sense of judgment operating within his own person. Guilt was the real evil in his own mental disorder. It was found in the isolation and estrangement that Boisen felt much of his life. There must be an abandonment of all disguises, the covert evil in the tyranny of shoulds, in order to discover a sense of justification and inner peace and fellowship. Boisen believed that the disorientation in mental illness is to be found in the isolation and estrangement people experience. It is often fear and guilt that results from the presence in one's life of that which one is afraid to tell, to confess. This is what Jungian analytical psychology calls the process of individuation

MYSTERY OF LIGHT RESTORATION TO A NEW VISION

What was his personal life like? His salary at Worcester amounted to about $3,500 annually. At that time the average salary of workers in the USA was $1,318. This $3,500 was the highest income he received for any given year. In 1924 the Congregational Home Missionary Society voted $50.00 a month.

He spent a good deal of his own money on the Council for Clinical Training. When he was at Elgin, he contributed about $1,000 a year from his estate income sent from Bloomington. He received full maintenance from the hospital, and he had limited needs personally.

When he moved to Elgin he lived a very Spartan life. He lived in a one-room apartment on the campus of Elgin State Hospital. He took many of his meals at the hospital cafeteria. He drove an old beat-up Ford automobile. Again, at Elgin his salary was around $3,000 a year.

He had no need to help support his mother who was living with his sister in Massachusetts. His mother had actually made it possible for him to take extra work at Harvard in the 1923-24. The Reverend Francis W. McPeek remembered when he was at Elgin that he occasionally received a check from Boisen to help with his student expenses. Boisen had taken out an insurance policy when he was at Union Seminary from 1908 to 1913, but he cancelled the policy after he left there. He saw no obligation to have an insurance policy. In 1952, he had approximately $200 in the bank as liquid assets.

There are books in the *Boisen Collection* at the Hammond Library that he willed to Chicago Theological Seminary. *First*, there are a number of the books on hymnody, general worship, and liturgy such as *Utilization of Music in Prisons and Mental Hospitals*. He collected a wide range of hymnals of various churches for study, most likely in conjunction with his own development of a hymnal for mental health facilities. *Second,* there were books on German literature, dictionaries, and textbooks for the teaching of German. Boisen had taught German and French for a brief period of time after college. He had several dictionaries and textbooks on the French language as well as those he must have used in his own teaching in high school. *Third,* there were many classical literary books in his personal library. There were books from *Beowulf* to a valuable edition of the complete works of William Shakespeare. There were books from his days in forestry about the care of trees, forestry in New England, and *Manual of Trees in North America,* for example. He had a special collection of the works of The Reverend Harry Emerson Fosdick. Classical literature included the *Iliad* and the *Odyssey,* the *Arabian Nights;* the *Divine Comedy* of Dante. He had a variety of major literature and historical figures. They included St. Francis's, *The Little Flowers,* St. Francis de Sales, Robert Louis Stevenson, Goethe's *Faust,* extracts of the *Chanson de Roland, The Lady of the Lake, King Henry the Fifth, History of the English Language,* the works of James Russell Lowell, poetry of Thomas Gray, Elizabeth Barrett Browning, Pearl Buck's *All Men are Brothers,* Browning's complete *Works, Saint Joan* by Shaw, *The Lyric Poems of Robert Burns, Aucassin and Nicolete* in French and *In Memoriam* by Alfred Lord Tennyson, to name a sample. He treasured the works of Ralph Waldo Emerson and had several of his writings, his lifelong friend Dr. William Lowe Bryan's *He Knew What was in a Man,* Hans Christian Anderson's *Fairy Tales,* his grandfather's *History of Indiana University,* The *Diagnostic and Statistical Manual: Mental Disorders,* a Bible, a biography of Rudyard Kipling, *The New Testament Condensed, The Poetical Works of William Wordsworth, Report on the Causes of Crime, 1931* and, two *Journal of Pastoral Care* copies. There were also works on psychology and human relations such as *Journey Towards Self-Realization, Depressed Class Psychology,* and the *Biology of Schizophrenia.* He had a very good literary, historical, and scientific reading collection. There was no one section of the library that dominated. He was a well rounded, well read man.[186]

There has been speculation regarding his use of a cane. In 1925, he developed arthritis in the right hip joint. He had a progressive severity of distress from the arthritis, eventually resulting in the need for a cane. His hip joint was completely ankhylosed [ankylosis is a stiffening of the joint to a permanent fusion] and, it did not get better. In other health complications, he also had recurring tonsillitis until his tonsils were removed when an adult. He had hernia surgery three times from 1935, 1940, and again in the late 1940s.

In his *Exploration of the Inner World,* Boisen acknowledged Sullivan's help with portions of the manuscript. Sullivan was at Sheppard and Enoch Pratt Hospital in Baltimore for 7½ years, December 1922-June 1930. When Sullivan was on staff, Boisen went to Sheppard and Enoch Pratt Hospital in Baltimore to see him, and he saw him many times thereafter. Sullivan cites Boisen as a significant Christian caregiver, and he felt his grasp of religious thoughts and techniques regarding the problem of schizophrenia were helpful to the psychiatrist and psychologist dealing with schizophrenia. In 1944 Sullivan came to Elgin State Hospital for a lecture series. He gave two lectures at Elgin Hospital and made a superb demonstration of his techniques of interviewing patients.[187]

Along with his schizophrenia, Boisen seems to have had what we would call in our twenty-first century, a social anxiety disorder which manifested itself in fear of social or public situations. As mentioned by Cedarleaf, McGiffert, and others, he had an intense self-consciousness in social settings. He had an unreasonable fear of embarrassment as well. He could do effective counseling at the hospital, for example, but he could not outside of the hospital. In the world of informality, he felt inferior and ashamed of his background; but, in the hospital, he was in charge. He could go and come in his own way, identifying with the hospital patients as a professional challenge. The sum and substance of this is that he just was not effective with normal people. With compassion, Dr. McGiffert said, "You can be a friend with people who are lopsided."

Carroll Wise had firsthand experience with Boisen for many years beginning in 1928. He succeeded Boisen at Worcester in 1932. He described him as being deferential, often bowing to you and others. He was very intensely involved in the movement. He had a part in starting the pastoral care education movement. His time, energy, and finances went into the movement. Carroll, as a student of Boisen's, remembered his participation in seminars as being very dogmatic. There were things you did not talk about. For example, you did not talk about the oedipal complex of Freud, childhood problems, the use of psychological language. If a student brought a personal problem to him, he would listen, and then admonish the student to resolve his/her own problems. He did not go into these issues with students. The existential situation was to be dealt with by the student. Carroll Wise was at Worcester when Boisen had his second breakdown, and he noticed him becoming intense, very dogmatic and nervous. Wise felt that all in all he was a very respectful person.[188]

The Reverend John Thomas told of another side of Boisen, an empathic, warm, and genuine side. In May 1942, Boisen was recruiting for the summer program that Rev. Don Beatty was going to supervise. Boisen came to McCormick Seminary in Chicago to talk with John and to let him know about Beatty. With some difficulty he climbed the steps of Fowler Hall, and he found John to tell him he needed to see Beatty. He then loaded John into his car and took him out to Elgin for an interview, taking him back to Chicago after the interview. Boisen was good at "doing something" for another that would enhance the clinical training program.[189] "Doing for" was not difficult, but "being for" was another matter.

There is a 1952 transcription made by The Reverend Francis W. McPeek who had been an outstanding student at Elgin State Hospital between summer of 1934 and the fall of 1936. Boisen kept up a longtime friendship with McPeek who was a Congregational pastor and chaplain, first at the National Training School for Boys in Washington, DC, and later Social Welfare Director of the Washington Federation of Churches. In 1958, he died suddenly at the age of 48 while serving as Executive Director of the Commission on Human Rights for the City of Chicago. The audio tape captures Boisen's personal affect.

The impression I get from listening to the audio tapes was that Boisen's affect was flat and dull. On the recording, he would pause a long time before responding to a question or comment. When he responded, he would answer the question directly and seldom add anything to the comment. He would say, "Yes, I agree." Or simply, "No," or "Might be," or a very brief remark would be made to a question posed by McPeek. The interviewer had to work hard to get responses from him despite the fact that they had been friends for a long time. When pressed, he did come forth, but it was tedious going. The times that Boisen was most willing to speak up, was in discussing case studies. Then, he spoke up with considerable energy and investment. McPeek had difficulty relating to Boisen, and also accepting his direction in the program.[190]

At Elgin Boisen would sit in seminars from 3 to 4. Sometimes he would fall asleep. He would wake up with a snort at 4:00 pm and go to supper. Otherwise he would often say nothing. "He was low key, anti-charismatic person. He lacked the skills of establishing, quickly, a warm close relationship with students."[191] His schizophrenia and sadness rendered him often as one distant and detached, even if he did not intend to be.

Again, psychologist Dr. Paul Pruyser, reflecting upon his meeting with Boisen, had similar recollections of Boisen's blunted affect. His expressiveness of face, voice tone, and gestures were diminished. However, this did not mean that he was not reacting to his environment or having feelings. Pruyser wrote, "The most outstanding feature of the man at the time I met him was his flat affect. There is an awful expression referring to chronic schizophrenic patients who have made a good hospital adjustment, or sometimes have been discharged and live on the outside. That expression is 'burnt out case.' The phrase came into my mind time and time again when I talked with him and saw him act. He was not without humor and delicacy, but something had happened in his feelings and their expression. I have always felt that his *Out of the Depths* conveys in its tone and selection of topics early the impression I gained in my personal confrontation with him. The language is beautiful, the topics are moving; but there is something utterly pathetic about it all. There is something of homesickness in it, ennobled by a sense of suffering. In his presence, I felt respect toward him, because of the cross he had to bear. But it was difficult to warm up to him for there was an odd distance between him and the rest of the world."[192] This served him well as a researcher, but had limits in his teaching and in building social relationships.

Personal Religious Life

As far as his personal religious life is concerned, he seldom followed a disciplined prayer and Bible reading program for the growth of his soul. He told The Reverend McPeek that he had been remiss in this. "The occasional has more meaning than the regular," he said. There was no formal practice of Bible study, but in preparation of sermons, classes, and lectures he made a good deal of the use of the Bible. He did write prayers for the hymnal liturgy he developed for the hospital setting. When he had a problem, he'd sit down and think about what God would have him do.

In preparation of a sermon, he would get a general idea of what he wanted to give. He would check to see whether he had used a particular sermon at that site on a prior occasion. Then, if it was a new theme, it meant going through a period of working things out. He usually started with a topical theme; then he went to a Biblical text. He'd try to discern what different impressions Jesus made in the life of his time. Of the sermons I have read, each had a Biblical reference and then a practical application to daily life.

For example, a sermon for the 12th of June 1932 had the theme, "Weeds." The Biblical text was Matthew 13:25, "While men slept, his enemy came and sowed tares among the wheat." He developed the theme by reference to "weeds in the crops of grain or other things of value"; and the necessity to deal with what we call weeds in our own life, our own personal garden. He then engaged the worshippers with four themes: (1. where weeds came from, (2. where weeds grew, (3 kinds of weeds, (4. what to do with weeds. He made personal application saying, "Notice that all that may be said about weeds applies also to certain habits or tendencies within us." The tendencies he names are strongly entrenched. They are especially strong in prosperous times and in individuals of great promise. What to do? "Put something worth while in place of them. He suggests two possibilities: *Discipline*, the denying of one's self in the unessential for the sake of the essential. *Plowing up and planting over* the meaning of some of the painful experiences of life.

A sermon for the seventh of March 1948 was about the Confession of Peter "You are the Christ, the Son of the living God." He developed the text around "What it meant to Jesus, and what it means to us." He brought in a common theme about the love of God. "The message of Christianity is that God is love, that with the eyes of love God looks not upon the eternal accomplishments but upon the motive, the heart, and that God is seeking to do for us above all that we ask or think." Boisen believed that divinity lies in all human beings. We only need to recognize it and claim it, for God is love and his love is for us. The theme, *God is love and his love is for all of us to claim* dominated many of Boisen's sermons and public expression of theology.

Love as the most significant aspect of Christianity was a focus of Liberal Theology in Boisen's day. This love of God was expressed in a sermon on the eighteenth of April 1952 where he declared that the heart of the Easter Message "is to be found in its message of love and in its picture of the kind of life that is to follow. It is a love that abides forever. All of the chasms bridged by a love that saw possibilities of usefulness in the wreckage of failure, of strength in instability and weakness." [193] In sermons, he was often ministering to himself as much as he was ministering to the others.

He felt that the story of Easter would be relevant to people in the mental hospital. Here is the risen Lord who is the answer to many of their particular problems in the sense of forgiveness. It was "casting out demons" that occupied much of Jesus' ministry of healing; and he saw the Easter experience as the triumph of salvation. It was the joy that came through pain, the life that came through death, the blessing that came through adversity, the love that came through sacrifice.

In the worship service, there was a sense of community, a shared experience of being a part of a greater whole that helped relieve the sense of isolation. The patients in the mental hospital have taken life seriously. The function of the worship is to recreate the moral insights of humankind at its very best. The service attempted to educate the conscience and reinforce the motives for victorious living.[194] "Dealing with problems in the presence of others helps to eliminate the sense of isolation which was the real evil in mental illness" he told Mc Peek in the interviews Mc Peek recorded in 1952. The sermon is of very great value to the patient. The most important role the sermon plays is to help the patient gain insight into what he or she faces. He tried to help the patient deal with his or her real problems and not to escape tribulations. He felt that what the patient faced in the hospital was not unlike what people in the ordinary congregation faced on a day-to-day basis; therefore preaching would not be too different whether in hospital or in a congregation in the community.

In the initial printing of the *Hymns of Hope and Courage*, The Reverend Dr. McFee Campbell raised the question of whether the "General Prayer of Confession" was not too morbid and tended to reinforce their feelings of guilt. Boisen thought it over carefully, consulting some others, and kept the General Confession as well as the 55th Psalm.

The Liturgy in Worship

In the liturgy, first, the General Confession is just that, it is a general one not just a personal one and it helped distribute the strain among others. Second, self blame is a damaging reaction rather than a malignant one. Boisen comments, that most of the people who blame themselves do get well, while those who blame others, who refused to face the situation within, tended not to get well. If we can help a patient accept responsibility for his (or her) own mistakes and to feel he (or she) is one with others, we are helping him (or her) along the way to health. It helped people know that they are not alone and others face the same issues. Boisen insisted that it is therapeutic to confess our sin. Sins are not only peculiar to just any one individual, but are peculiar to the whole human race.

The Assurance of Pardon follows the General Confession. The Assurance of Pardon is also a way of joining in the promises and hopes that God has for humankind. Boisen believed that the role of the minister was to represent the "society at its best," and to give assurance grounded in the care of the soul and psychological insights. "The service of worship has been the outstanding example of group therapy throughout the centuries. It has helped people to think and feel together regarding the things that are most worthwhile. And that is the essence of group therapy, it seems. Confession is the basis, the essence of all psychotherapy; and it is the function of the therapist to forgive and accept the patient."[195] In the worship service, Boisen called upon the traditional music and liturgy of the church to provide ministry to the patients and staff of the hospital. Absolution can be informal in a therapy session while it is formalized in a worship service. Boisen was saying that whether formal or informal, confession and absolution are essential in a helping relationship.

The Reverend John Lennart Cedarleaf wrote about his first CPE experience at Elgin Hospital with Boisen. "On the seventh day," Cedarleaf wrote, "we were back as observers of the hospital chapel service." Boisen's words describe the seventh day. He told the students that at the service of worship on Sunday they would be using his *Hymns of Hope and Courage* that had met with criticism because it was deemed too high brow. Boisen said: "I believe in the principles on which it is built. I am convinced that words count and that religious belief is more likely to be affected by hymns than by sermons. For patients who are desperately grasping for Ultimate Reality, it is of utmost importance that the religious services bring suggestions which are wholesome and constructive."[196] Music does a very good job of creating the sense of oneness. In the compilation of a hymnal was his belief that the service of worship was an outstanding example of group therapy. In an article entitled, "The Service of Worship in a Mental Hospital: Its Therapeutic Significance," that appeared in the *Journal of Clinical Pastoral Work*, Volume 2, No 1, (1948) he wrote "The therapeutic significance of the service of worship can best be understood in the light of George Mead's theory that the personality is the internalization within the individual of the group organization by means of language." Boisen believed, as did George Mead, that symbols [language] "arouse in us the same response as they do in others. The personality is thus a set of social responses that have become organized and habituated." The social response then is not just to others in general but to those we love and admire whose authority we accept, those who for religious man/woman are associated with the idea of God. "In the case of the assembly of the Christian Church," he goes on, "this represents to the believer the fellowship of the best. And its meetings are designed to keep alive the loyalty to each other and the common loyalty to God whom the worshippers regard as the source of their life, the controller of their destiny, and the one to whom they owe unreserved allegiance."[197]

Some of the criteria for rejecting hymns were:

1. Reference to enemies and concern about enemies was a malignant reaction that needed no fostering.
2. Materials likely to reinforce the belief in the authority of

'voices' and other subconscious promptings; e.g. "Christians do you see them?" and "Speak that I may speak."

3. Materials likely to reinforce belief in the magical, e.g. "There is a fountain filled with blood" and "Rock of Ages cleft for me."

4. Material likely to intensify a sense of helplessness, fear, or isolation. e.g. "Once to everyman and nation," and "Before Jehovah's awful throne."

5. Materials out of keeping with the situation and mood of those patients in a mental hospital, e.g. "Rejoice you pure in heart," and "Joyful, joyful, we adore Thee."

Some criteria for including hymns were:

1. Musical lyrics giving expression of the consciousness of sin and need for a better life.

2. Materials portraying love and forgiveness by God.

3. Lyrics giving expression to attitudes of resignation and attitudes of faith.

4. Expressions of courage and action.

5. Hymns of the future life.

6 Hymns adapted to special purposes and occasions: Christmas, New Year, Easter, and Eucharist.[198]

He generally led the worship himself, except when students came on board, they could take a turn at leading in worship and have their peers critique the service. Following Dr. George Herbert Mead's theory of language,[199] Boisen felt that the words of the hymns really mattered. Tunes were important, but their function was to reinforce the words and serve as an aid to recall. A number of the hymns, traditionally in a Protestant hymnbook, did not apply at all to the experiences of the patients. Consideration of the words of the hymns was especially made.[200]

To worship was to get in contact with feelings in relation to God, in relation to self, in relation to others, and in touch with the religious environment that nurtures and sustains one another. However, religious emotion was not to be looked upon as an end in itself, but as a means of remaking and stabilizing character. What was important to Boisen was the behavior sequences that were impacted by the hymn, or the prayer, or the sermon, or the sacrament.

After working for more than a year on an appropriate selection of hymns, psalms, and prayers, in 1926 he published a hymnal entitled *Lift Up Your Hearts* with revisions in 1932, 1937 and 1950 under the title *Hymns of Hope and Courage*. He liked to have hymns that dealt constructively with the problems with which the patients were facing, hymns that would help them face the things themselves and to do so in the light of the best Christian doctrine. He liked hymns with literary value, too. In the course of four editions, the pitch for singing was lowered to accommodate a general congregation. In the *Foreword* to the 1950 edition he wrote: "This book is intended for those who are passing through the valley of conflict and shadow. It produces a compact collection of hymns, prayers, and passages of Scripture designed to deepen the aspirations for a better life, to strengthen faith in the love and healing power of God and to foster attitudes of hope and courage."[201] In the hymnbook there is an Order of Service, Prayers for Special Occasions, and Responsive Readings from the scriptures, and then a careful selection of 108 hymns.

ANTON THEOPHILUS BOISEN:

Second Episode of Mental Illness 1930

Boisen had his second episode of mental illness and hospitalization in 1930, precipitated by the death of his mother. This episode lasted for three weeks. His psychiatrist was Milton H. Erickson, MD who emphasized Boisen's problem as a disorder of thought rather than of affect. Robert Powell, MD, PhD, a contemporary psychiatrist interested in Boisen, said that "although there undoubtedly were excessively affective components to Boisen's behavior during his disturbed episodes, one may feel some confidence in his self diagnosis of 'dementia praecox.'"[202]

The Reverend Carroll Wise recalled the event of Boisen's hospitalization: "In 1930, I went to Worcester to be his Assistant. I lived through this break in 1930 that occurred after the death of his mother. He seemed less composed when I arrived, certainly less than the previous summer. Also, his relationship with Alice was not altogether smooth. Then, there was a very aggressive woman in the Worcester clinical pastoral education group. She was in conflict with him from the first day, and would attack him in the seminars. In private he would talk to me about her. He felt himself inadequate to cope with such an aggressive woman. He put women on a high pedestal where they could not relate to him. When the program was over, he left the Chaplaincy work to me; and he went to Chicago to visit his friends at C T S. He returned in early October, and I met him at the Railroad Station. He wanted to be admitted to the hospital. He wanted to spend time in his office, and he wanted me to stay with him.

"During the short trip to the hospital, he was preoccupied. After we were settled in his office, he began talking. First he wanted assurances that I would be loyal to him. He told me that I occupied a special place in his scheme of things. Then he unfolded a series of ideas that we had heard him discuss before in relation to the case histories of patients."

"The world was facing a great catastrophe, but all was not lost. He revealed that he had a great part to play in restoring order. He was in line with the prophets, John Bunyan, George Fox, and Jesus. I was to be the son he never had. Then he repeated an idea he'd spoken of before. That sex was much more than an individual matter. It had social and cosmic significance. He felt he had failed greatly as he had not married, and he did not have a son. When he died, the Boisen name would go out of use as a famous name. He was the last, and his great failure was that he did not continue the family name. This had some relationship to his ideas of the 'family of four.' To bring harmony back into the world, I was to be his son. The clinical training movement would be the agency through which we would work. This had all been revealed to him. This was followed by a story of great guilt and depression. He had committed what to him was the most abominable sin - masturbation. He deserved to be castrated. Self destructive fantasies came out strongly. I confess I got frightened. Boisen lived by himself in a rooming house in the city of Elgin. It was not difficult to visualize him performing a self destructive act. It was not difficult to see him becoming violent toward others. He would be a hard man to handle, especially in a psychotic condition - What to do?"

Dr. William A. Bryan, the Director of Worcester State Hospital,[203] knew how to handle Boisen. Dr. Bryan knew you had to be very firm with people like him. He had the ability to be firm. Though getting late, I asked Anton to allow me to call Dr. Bryan at his apartment and invite him to come to see us. He agreed because he felt that Dr. Bryan had a place to play in his new system of ideas. Dr. Bryan was out, and would be returning late. I left an emergency call. He did call and came over. The three of us went over Boisen's story, and it was well after midnight when I took Boisen to his room. He had promised Dr. Bryan that he would be quiet in his room and would not harm himself. Dr Bryan's confidence in Boisen's promise had a very quieting effect; some therapy had been done that night, right there. In the several weeks following, I spent time with Dr. Bryan and others, in making decisions. Our first attempt was to try to keep him from being committed to the hospital, though this was a calculated risk.

"As a young neophyte, I learned much about how to handle such people. Especially in the relationship I bore to him. I spent hours in his office, listening. I learned about the ideas he presented in seminars and his own inner conflicts. He told me that the real magnitude of guilt was the sense of isolation. Here was a man, profoundly isolated, alienated, feeling rejected by others. These were deep feelings and they could not be handled by any of the superficial techniques that we have developed today."[204]

Wise had made time to talk with Boisen each day, during which time he gained respect for this troubled man. Then one day Dr. Helen Flanders Dunbar came to visit. He had asked for her specifically. They were together some time. She left without saying a word. From that day on he was better.[205] Dr. Robert Powell believed that Boisen's feelings for Helen Dunbar went deeper than professional admiration. It does seem that there is a very special emotional attachment to Flanders Dunbar that Boisen never revealed even in his autobiography.[206]

MYSTERY OF LIGHT RESTORATION TO A NEW VISION

Courtesy Hammond Library Boisen Collection CTS

Helen Flanders Dunbar, A.B., M.A., B. D., M.D., Ph.D.

Dr. Dunbar was a brilliant intellectual with a precocious professional perspective on religion and human behavior. Dr. Dunbar believed that cooperation between the physician (science) and the priest (religion) was important. Her Ph.D. dissertation (1929) on *Symbolism in Medieval Thought and its Consummation in the "Divine Comedy"* was acclaimed in Dante studies. She used biblical references to her interpretation of Dante's work, and proclaimed that "religion and science are not antagonistic but complementary through symbolism."[207]

She wrote, "If cooperation [with the various disciplines of medicine] is important for the physician of the body it is no less important for the theologian who feels himself the physician of the soul? "[208] Dr. Dunbar had an approach to the individual that was to try to set the person's mind at ease, to get the patient to think for himself/herself. She wrote:

"Few patients need to be given advice as to what to do once they are emotionally free to think. The true reformer must be like the man in Plato's *Allegory of the Cave* who knew that his chief task was to turn the prisoners [watching the shadows on the back of the cave] around so that they could face the direction of the sun, the real world sources of the shadows. We need only show patients or parishioners the way out of the cave, once they see the path clearly before them they can be trusted to take it."[209]

Interest in Mysticism

When Boisen got acquainted with Dr. Dunbar's theories on medieval mysticism, he became interested in mysticism and the relationship to mental health. For a month, Flanders Dunbar had been in Boisen's first student unit during summer of 1925 at which time she was studying at Columbia University and the nearby Union Theological Seminary and was about to enter Yale Medical School. Dr. Dunbar's Ph.D. dissertation at Columbia University was on "Symbolism in Medieval Thought and Its Consummation in the *Divine Comedy*." Boisen kept a picture of Dante in his room. He felt that there was something very important about the exceptional mental and religious states of the great religious leaders in human history, the testimony that substantiates the moving power within the human being that makes for righteousness and human wholeness. The quest in the 12th and 13th century medieval romance literature and song depicted the seeker, a knight, prince, king, buffoon on a journey of discovery, a discovery of oneness with God, and religious redemption, best symbolized in Chrèstien de Troyes' *Perceval and the Story of the Grail* in 12th century medieval literature. The journey was often long and arduous, painful and death-defying; but in the end the sojourner emerged with a sense of wholeness.[210]

Boisen claimed to have a direct mystical encounter with God that became his "guiding intelligence." This was his source of new ideas and insights and more than just rearranging of old ideas.[211] The term mystical for Boisen meant the "sense of identification with the superhuman."[212] This experience was the fountainhead of religion. The method of inducing exceptional mental and spiritual states was a narrowing of attention and autosuggestion. This was accomplished through self-hypnosis, methods of repetitive, constant self-affirmations.[213] Boisen contended that in religious geniuses, he found a companionship to his soul. He referred to significant mystics such as St. Paul, John Fox, Madame Guyon, John Bunyan, Saint Teresa of Avila, and Emanuel Swedenborg as models that enabled him to cope with life's struggles and come through.

In research with patients with schizophrenia conducted by students the conclusion was that the sense of mystical identification is found in those cases in which the patient is grappling desperately with a threat to his/her integrity and is brought face to face with what for her/him is ultimate reality.[214] Boisen believed that at the very center of a constellation of ideas that are found in the schizophrenic patient are found also in many of the important religious leaders. His favorites were: David Brainerd, a Presbyterian working with the Delaware Indians of Eastern Pennsylvania, New York, and New Jersey during the early eighteenth century; John Bunyan, a Puritan Separatist preacher of seventeenth century England whose *Pilgrim's Progress* became a religious classic; George Fox founder of the Religious Society of Friends (Quakers) in England of the seventeenth century; Søren Kierkegaard, a Danish theologian the nineteenth century and father of existential theology, Heinrick Suso, a Dominican friar of the fourteenth century; Saint Teresa of Avila, a Spanish Carmelite contemplative of the sixteenth century; Madame Guyon, a French, Catholic mystic (1648 to 1717); Emanuel Swedenborg (1688-1772) a renowned scientist of the Enlightenment and explorer of the physical world, who through an intense soul-filled conversion experienced the gift of religious wisdom and became an originator of the religious correspondences of human inner space; and not to be over-looked was Dante Alighieri, a thirteenth-century Italian who wrote the classic *The Divine Comedy*. These writers did not all have the same mystical experiences; however, they do depict passing through a period of acute conflict, often likened to a state of profound darkness, and at a "tipping point" discovering an integrated faith and selfhood, a new light on life and the Holy. Boisen often equated conversion to a mystical-like experience. [215]

In *Out of the Depths* he wrote about ideas of self sacrifice, of death, of world disaster, of mystical identification with birth and rebirth, of reincarnation, of prophetic mission are to be found not only in his case but in other acutely disturbed schizophrenics. As he had shown elsewhere, such ideas seem to form a sort of constellation which is distinctive of acute schizophrenics. Therefore, such ideas have meaning.[216]

Early, Dr. Helen Flanders Dunbar was very active in the Council for Clinical Training of Theological Students, first as Medical Director and then Executive Director. Professor Edward Thornton wrote that Dunbar's leadership of the Council for Clinical Training was authoritarian. "She was cold and calculating, non-communicative, and basically rather shy. All the young ministers who worked with her found it necessary to struggle against her manipulative ways. They were fascinated, however, by her political adroitness, her somewhat cynical view of established values and important people. They were committed to her because of her intense commitment to the cause of relating the clergy to physicians in a constructive way and because of her genuine religious interest."[217]

By early spring of 1932, Boisen decided to take leave of Worcester, and we find him next at the edge of the prairie.

12

GOING WEST TO ELGIN STATE HOSPITAL

Boisen left Worcester State Hospital to take a position at Elgin State Hospital near Chicago on the 1st of April 1932. Elgin was a large state mental hospital with approximately 5,000 patients. This population was served by 24 physicians and a large staff of attendants. Boisen's title was Acting Chaplain of the Hospital. He was in charge of a program of research into the religious factors in mental illness. There was a provision at Elgin State Hospital for two advanced students, or fellows as they were called, who could come for a whole year of training. These students were given a salary of $75 a month and full maintenance. There was also a place for a student who came for a period of not less than three months, mainly in the summer. Elgin was opened as a training center for clinical pastoral education on April 6, 1932.

It was not easy to cut loose from Worcester. He had been at Worcester eight years. His undertaking developed from a very small beginning to a movement that had become national. He left the work at Worcester to the competent leadership of The Reverend Carroll Wise. In a brochure for Elgin State Hospital Boisen describes Elgin's peculiar position as the oldest training center both among the centers of the CPE Council for Clinical Training and the Institute for Pastoral Care. However, it was not connected to either of the major associations because of special difficulties rooted in his idiosyncrasies and his disagreement with some of the developments in the first decade of the pastoral care and education movement.

The inquiry into the meaning of the patient's experience was an integral part of training Dynamic versus genetic interpretations, purposes, meanings, values. The program sought to develop interpersonal relations and theological consideration versus "oral, anal, and genital stages of development" (Freud). Therapeutic benefit to the student was a by-product of the effort to understand and help the patient. The method at Elgin was an empirical approach, with a research social scientist, to the ancient problems of sin and salvation. This approach was, later, viewed as a major contribution to theological education.

Being at Elgin made it possible for Boisen to be closer to Chicago Theological Seminary where he continued to lecture as a Research Associate in the Psychology of Religion Department. He was also close to Alice who worked in Chicago. Soon after his arrival at Elgin, he established the Chicago Council for Clinical Training that was loosely affiliated with the Council for Clinical Training of Theological Students in New York. Chicago had ten "Class-A theological schools" making it, at that time, the largest consortium of theological schools in the world. The program Boisen fostered through the Chicago Council for Clinical Training of Theological Students aimed to address theological education at the point of what Boisen considered its greatest weakness, the on hands empirical approach to the other (patient, parishioner, client, and grieving spouse). It provided an opportunity to study theology, under guidance, using the raw material of human life and thus to do for theological education what the introduction of the case method and the clinical internship did for medical education.[218]

He felt that the project was now safely launched. There were eight students in the summer program in 1932; four were from McCormick Theological Seminary (Presbyterian), two from Chicago Theological Seminary (Congregational), one from Western Theological Seminary (Reformed Church in America), and one from Meadville Seminary (Unitarian). He was very gratified by the attendance and response to the religious worship services, some of which he led and others were led by the students. When he arrived the worship services were conducted by local clergy who tended to use their own Sunday morning sermon for the congregation at the mental hospital. This meant that the sermon usually did not relate well to the patients. There were about seventy patients coming when he arrived and within a year more than one hundred seventy were regularly attending worship services. He also introduced the newly revised hymnal for use in the hospital. He was both surprised and delighted on how the congregation took hold of the service and the singing was great. He had a choir of some thirty individuals, some of whom were very good singers.

Boisen had begun a journey that would occupy the remainder of his long life. His was essentially an inward motivated quest. It was developed from within outward, providing dynamically and functionally for his leadership of the pastoral care and education movement. Boisen's educational endeavor was content centered. He used extensive case histories that involved the patient's narrative story.

By 1932, a rift had already begun within the movement. After Boisen's 1930 hospitalization, Dr. Richard Cabot no longer trusted Boisen's judgment and leadership; and a break occurred between the two. Cabot would have little to do with those who alleged that mental illness was due to inner psychiatric pathology. He rejected the claim of Boisen that a "breakthrough" had occurred between the science of medicine and religion. For Boisen, the move to Elgin was heavily motivated by the contemptuous relationship between himself and Rev. Austin Philip Guiles.

13

A RIFT WITH THE COUNCIL FOR CLINICAL TRAINING AND CONTINUANCE OF BOISEN'S JOURNEY

From the early stages of the development of the clinical pastoral education movement, Boisen was in sharp divergence with some of the members of both the Council for Clinical Training and also the Boston group that eventually became the Institute for Pastoral Care. The Council was formed on January 21, 1930 in the home of Samuel Eliot, pastor of the Unitarian Church of Boston. The Council, in 1932, moved the headquarters to New York City with Helen Flanders Dunbar, MD, as Executive Director with absolute authority. The Council stressed the value of experience in the mental hospital together also with that in the general hospital and in the correctional institutions.

The Reverend Dr. Philip Guiles was at odds with both Anton Boisen and Dr. Helen Flanders Dunbar. He left the Council in 1931 and was hired on staff as the first full-time professor in psychology and clinical studies at Andover-Newton Seminary in 1932. The

Boston group, under the leadership of Dr. Richard Cabot and The Reverend Dr. Philip Guiles formed New England Theological Schools Committee on Clinical Training in 1938 that became the Institute of Pastoral Care in 1944. It devoted attention toward general hospitals with the Institute centered in seminaries. Their training emphasis was upon skill and ability to deal with people in trouble. The nature, purpose, and location of clinical pastoral education (in seminaries) differed markedly from the Council for Clinical Training. However, there was full agreement in regard to the need of the empirical approach to the study of religious experience.

After Boisen's hospitalization in 1930 he was made a consultant.[219] Edward Thornton points out: "He was on the periphery of the activity of the Council in New York from the beginning in 1930 to his death."[220] In 1939, Boisen officially withdrew his involvement altogether from the national office of the Council for Clinical Training. He concentrated on the Council he had formed in the Chicago area as an autonomous organization.

Boisen was a close friend with Dr. Helen Flanders Dunbar. Under Dr. Dunbar's leadership, the Council had moved to New York City. Reverend Philip Guiles was the Field Representative for the Council beginning in 1930; however, Guiles was unable to get along with Dr. Dunbar who was chosen Executive Director of the newly formed Council. Guiles took the position that the Council had to decide between himself and Dr. Dunbar for leadership. The Council chose Dr. Dunbar. Subsequently, Guiles moved to Massachusetts and became a faculty member at Andover-Newton Seminary and a partner with Dr. Richard Cabot.

As Executive Director of the Council, Dr. Dunbar emphasized three basic standards for programs:

1. To develop a program that would guarantee a student's discovering his or her distinctive role as a minister in relation to the health care community;
2. To avoid the introduction of psychoanalytic technique in a student's clinical training;
3. To provide in every training center dual supervision by a graduate trained in theology and supervision and a staff adviser qualified to give the point of view of the institution.

Clinical training was focused on the minister involved in learning the art of soul care and theological reflection. However, by the late forties and early fifties, the Council had moved away from the standard to "avoid the introduction of psychoanalytic technique in a student's clinical training." [221]

Background for the move to New England is related to a "falling out" not only with Guiles and Dunbar but also between Guiles and Boisen. It was representative of a similar falling out Boisen had with Dr. Richard Cabot when sides were drawn. In 1932, when Philip Guiles was invited to become a member of the faculty of Andover-Newton Seminary, he made the Seminary separate from the Council, "but a related venture." Cabot and Guiles ended up in New England, Boisen and Dunbar in New York.

The explanation for the rift, from Boisen's point of view, is contained in a letter Boisen had written to Dr. Willard L. Sperry, Dean of Harvard Divinity School, on December 6, 1933. Dr. Sperry had inquired of Guiles. It was a letter that frankly set forth what Boisen called "unhappy differences" between Guiles and the Council, and Guiles and Boisen.

Boisen had had a prior experience with Philip Guiles when he came to Worcester State Hospital for training in 1928. It was not more than a month into the program that Guiles took a violent dislike to Reverend Donald Beatty, Boisen's very capable assistant. Boisen tried hard to help them overcome their differences, but failed. He wrote that Guiles could be "charming, enthusiastic, untiring in his eagerness to help people in distress, full of ideas, gifted with wisdom and imagination and a veritable artist in his ability to interest others in the things in which he is interested. On the other hand, he was dominated all too often by a will-to-power that makes it difficult for him to do team work. He is apt to be particularly antagonistic to all those who are in any way rivals and who thus threaten his security."

Boisen's comment about Guiles continued to intensify. He accused him of raising a fund to send him to Europe for a year when he was discharged from his hospitalization in 1930. While Boisen was in hospital, Guiles took over the summer program at Worcester. Boisen returned to Worcester but Guiles and Dr. Cabot did not want him to assume his education work. With the support of Superintendent Bryan, he did return to resume full duties in charge of pastoral care and supervising. This made a difficult situation for Boisen and Guiles that neither of them managed well. Feelings were intense between the two. Boisen believed that his move to Elgin in 1932 was the only way out for him. It also sealed the break between Guiles and Dunbar. Reverend Carroll Wise took over when Boisen left Worcester.

After Boisen was at Elgin State Hospital, he made an effort to find an understanding with Guiles to end the misunderstanding so they could continue to work together in the movement. This, too, was an unhappy idea. Boisen admitted that two people of outstanding ability, whose particular qualifications supplemented each other admirably, are now at variance with each other. This undertaking springs out of the religious motive that Guiles is interested in setting up church clinics or setting up as a psychotherapist, while

A RIFT WITH THE COUNCIL FOR CLINICAL TRAIN-ING

Boisen has insisted that the first application of the insights gained through the hospital experience be to the minister's message and to his/her work as a pastor. Therefore, that message was to be theological, not psychological. Boisen developed this difference in his letter to Sperry, a point that had already been made as Boisen's point of view. His difficulty was with a person like Guiles or those who followed the psychological track at the Council. Guiles was, however, the first clinically trained person appointed to a full-time position on a theological faculty. [222]

The Reverend Dr. Frederic Norstad, a Lutheran student of Guiles, said of his supervisor: "Phil was not completely accepted by the Institute because he was very psychoanalytically oriented."[223]

Dr. Seward Hiltner joined the Council administration in 1935 and stayed until 1938. Dunbar had left the Council, and during years of Seward Hiltner, there was a period of a basic commitment to a professional model for theological education, a model that equipped seminarians for effective pastoral work. "Hiltner sought to create a research community dedicated to empirical inquiry into the religious dimension of life."[224]

Boisen was also concerned that the methods for learning begin with the empirical approach. He criticized the method of beginning with the systematized preconceptions found in textbooks. In these principles, Boisen felt that Guiles was going in another direction. Philip Guiles had become an enthusiastic adherent of psychoanalysis. He was setting up clinics and doing psychoanalysis without ever qualifying as an analyst. This seemed to Boisen to be very unwise, and it risked a potential ethical conflict with the medical profession. Both Boisen and Dr. Dunbar were opposed to the direction Guiles was taking in developing clinics and did not want them under their auspices.[225]

The Reverend Robert Brinkman, who followed Hiltner as

ANTON THEOPHILUS BOISEN:

Executive from1938–1948, was very interested in depth psychology. Also, when Reverend Fred Kuether became Executive Director of the Council beginning in 1948, he was interested in focusing on personal relationships. Boisen's heirs, among the New York group, after Hiltner left in l938, became invested in the depth psychologies. Boisen was more focused on research into the religious aspects of mental illness as a theologian. He was less interested in the student's feelings and more in the various aspects of the patient's narrative as material for theological reflection.

The Council for Clinical Training was a disappointment to Boisen. It had placed its main emphasis upon early childhood conditions and upon techniques of counseling and group work. The central focus for the student in theological education was not being asked, and good methods of cooperative inquiry were not being developed.[226] Boisen also questioned the development of Standards for the Council that dismissed a person like Granger Westberg. He wrote: "we will not recognize him because he has not met our Standards. He is, an unusually able and attractive fellow who took the Chaplaincy at Augustana Hospital in Chicago. He had had six months training, most of it with Russell Dicks."[227] However, he did not meet the Standards for a supervisor with the Council for Clinical Training, Standards with which Boisen found himself at variance and hard pressed to meet.

In the early thirties, a major schism in the movement was precipitated by the encounters, feelings, pride, and daring of The Reverends Anton Boisen and Austin Philip Guiles and two physicians, Doctors Helen Flanders Dunbar and Richard Cabot. The rift continued to exist until the merger of clinical training programs in 1967 when the Association for Clinical Pastoral Education, Inc. was given birth.

A RIFT WITH THE COUNCIL FOR CLINICAL TRAIN-ING
Mental Breakdown 1935

In 1935, Boisen had yet another mental breakdown, and this time he was hospitalized at Sheppard and Enoch Pratt Hospital in Baltimore, Maryland. Alice Batchelder had told him she had cancer of the breast and that death was imminent. It was this thought of her illness that brought about the train of ideas and carried him off into the same little known country which he had previously visited. He told the doctors, "It remains my deliberate judgment, and I must be true to the purpose manifest in the disturbed period, I still have faith in the love that has determined my life for 33 years as that which is best in this life of mine, and I am ready to give all to be true to that love."[228] Alice died on December 2, 1935. He was unable to attend her funeral because of his hospitalization.

In the medical record at Sheppard and Enoch Pratt Hospital in Baltimore, it is stated that during this hospitalization he was at times very alone and at other times he tried to help other patients by asking them about their lives. On several occasions, during the night he got up, dressed himself, began singing loudly, and had to be sent to a more disturbed ward. He quieted down after several weeks, and he wrote a good many letters, cooperated with the hospital personnel, worked in occupational therapy, and made plans for his departure. He wrote a long letter of appeal for discharge to Dr. Noble, dated 10 December 1935. He wanted to be discharged to assume his teaching duties at Chicago Theological Seminary, his only means of income at that time. His plan was to leave the hospital on Sunday and resume teaching a course with Dr. Cushman McGiffert on Tuesday.[229]

This had been the fourth time he had suffered a schizophrenic breakdown in the last 15 years. "They came on quite abruptly and were characterized by the same general ideation. They would clear up and leave no ill effects." As a matter of fact, some of his best work was done in the weeks following a hospitalization.

His discharge was delayed until December 16, 1935 when he left the hospital. One month after admission, it was noted that "the patient has shown considerable improvement. He is now free from delusion; though he maintained a slightly tense and uneasy attitude." He had been expressing frequently the desire to return to his teaching at the seminary in Chicago without resuming his hospital work, the hospital work to be cared for by his associate Donald Beatty. He had a full recovery and did not have another episode until near the time of his death. He returned to teaching at Chicago Theological Seminary and to his chaplaincy and supervisor's responsibility at Elgin after the first of the year, 1936.[230]

Co-operative Inquiry

In another letter to The Reverend Fred Kuether, Executive Director for the Council for Clinical Training, dated the 21 September 1948, in a full and frank statement, Boisen shared his disagreement with the philosophy of teaching that had developed in the Council for Clinical Training. "The chief difference, as I see it, lies in your view that research into the religious aspects of mental illness and other disabilities is a secondary matter; and that research and training are to be kept separate. According to my philosophy, in all good teaching, student and teacher alike are engaged in *co-operative inquiry* and the best possible conditions for effective teachings are to be found when they are actually participating in a project of real significance. From the beginning, therefore, I have stressed the significance of mental illness and the challenge that it brings to the student of religion, and I have looked upon the students as fellow explorers of a 'little-known country.'"

In another letter to Fred Kuether, he voiced his disappointment with The Reverend William Andrew, the chaplain that succeeded him at Elgin State Hospital in 1945. That summer, Boisen had already selected Professor Wayne Oates and five of his Louisville Southern Baptist students, and Professor Jesse Ziegler and five of his students from Bethany Seminary in Chicago. They had come to Elgin expecting to have Boisen as their supervisor. This was a disappointment for both Oates and Ziegler. It was also a difficult summer for Bill Andrew having students he himself had not selected.

Rev. Andrew did not follow Boisen's style of teaching. He dealt not only with theological reflection but also with the feelings of patients and students about their peer and professional relationships. This method of learning required a relatively safe environment. He used Wilhelm Reich's *Character Analysis* and mentioned to students Reich's book on *Orgone Therapy*.[231] Given Boisen's sexual maladjustments and sexual fixation in his case studies and his personal life, it is not difficult to believe he conflicted with Bill Andrew who drew upon the Freudian and Reichian approach, and who was more interested in the personal emotional and religious formation of the student than was Boisen.

In further correspondence with The Reverend Fred Kuether, Boisen voiced his opposition to the Council again. This time it was another issue. He wrote, "My chief objection is that the Council had become too much a 'peer court.' By that I mean a close-knit, same aged, group which develops its own standards. But you have nonetheless accomplished something of great value, and you have done so in the face of many difficulties and dislodgements." *Common Neuroses of Children and Adults,* by O. Spurgeon English and Gerald H. J. Pearson, had become the gospel in many of the Council centers.

In the same letter, he again pointed out a clear difference in his method of teaching and that of a majority of the Council Centers and supervisors. "I have proceeded upon the assumptions that in dealing objectively with the problem of people in trouble the student gets invaluable help in dealing with his difficulties. It has been my policy to trust the student to work out his own problems except as he comes to me for help. I have taken no little time for personal conferences with students." This philosophy of respect for the student's process continued to be a thread in his work with students at Worcester and at Elgin State Hospital.[232] He strongly opposed the fact that Clinical Pastoral Education had become, in several centers, personal therapy for students.

In another long letter to Fred Kuether upon the occasion of Fred's resignation as Executive Director of the Council for Clinical Training in 1954, [233] Boisen was more candid regarding the "program of inquiry" of the Council. He wrote, "Herein lays the Council's chief deficiency. It has failed to develop a program of inquiry. Instead of asking significant questions and developing methods of inquiry which will stand up under scrutiny, the emphasis has been placed upon techniques of counseling. With this, I have no quarrel. It has been perhaps, a healthy reaction against my own over-emphasis on inquiry. What I do object to is the fact that Freudian dogma has been accepted on faith and even made basic in a standardized curriculum. And instead of centering attention upon the patient and his problems, with personal therapy as a by-product, the prevailing tendency seems to be to center attention upon the students. Students getting psychoanalyzed seemed to have become a requirement, unwritten but none the less real; and group therapy, where it is practiced, has sometimes been concerned with the student other than with the patients."[234]

A RIFT WITH THE COUNCIL FOR CLINICAL TRAIN-ING
World War II

During the Second World War Boisen wrote an article that was printed in *Psychiatry* entitled, "Conscientious Objectors, and their Morale in Church-Operated Service Units." This was written for the Brethren Church and the American Friends Service Committee who had Conscientious Objectors as mental health workers in their facilities during WW II. Also, the morale and the cooperation of workers in the Civilian Public Service camps had become a matter of concern to the supporting churches. The need for channeling of aggression was the chief factor in the development of better morale in hospital units over against service camps.

For example, in upper Minnesota's lumbering region, there were conscientious objectors whose lack of channeling aggression found its way into bad behavior. The result of this behavior was the "draining off" of the best men into other jobs. A large number were discharged because of their antagonistic and general malingering attitude. Boisen recommended that "trouble makers should not be rewarded by being discharged for return to their community. Such a policy may solve the immediate problem of what to do with a particular recalcitrant but it encourages further reactions of this type." He also urged that the camp be regarded as primarily a clearing house for individuals to find placement further down the line.[235]

His friend of long-standing, Dr. William Lowe Bryan, who was now retired President of Indiana University, wrote, "I am glad to receive your paper on Conscientious Objectors. Christians are in a hard place between their desire to follow the teachings of Christ and the conditions which seem to force them to war. It is not surprising that many make the decision, to renounce war, under whatever circumstances."[236] In an article published in *Social Action* of the Congregational Church, he had written about the Holiness religious groups that grew in the 1930s because of the Great Depression. As they felt together intensely about the things that matter most, Boisen believed the principle was that, by in large, during crises periods there is a quickening of religious interest more so than during traditional religious times of celebrating, such as a coming of age, getting married, having children, bereavement, and death. "War increases the sense of fellowship, brings forth heroic devotion, and compels men and women to do fresh and earnest thinking." He found it difficult to say why this did not carry over into constructive religious movements. The deepened sense of fellowship that war engenders seemed often confined to the "in group." War breeds hatred, and hatred bars the door to love and truth. He contended that the Hebrew-Christian religion had something to teach us in the matter of dealing with the problem of war, not merely in defeat but also in victory.

The Reverend John Thomas remembered that in 1947, it was the Council's idea to have Boisen be a consultant and encouraged him to visit the Council centers. It was virtually "kicking him upstairs." Clinical training in the Council had moved beyond Boisen's practice of it, and the newer supervisors were exploring new methods of training and supervision. He was never certified by the Council. [237] Boisen traveled considerably and addressed various CPE gatherings and theological seminaries while being a faculty member at Chicago Theological Seminary and Chaplain at Elgin State Hospital. In February of 1943 he had traveled to Berkeley, California to spend time on the campus of the Pacific School of Religion. He was one of the lecturers at the Pacific School of Religion on the invitation of Dr. Arthur Cushman McGiffert Jr., at that time the President of the seminary. He gave lectures in the prestigious series of the Earl Lectures. He also stimulated interest in clinical pastoral education for seminary students in the Bay area seminaries.

A RIFT WITH THE COUNCIL FOR CLINICAL TRAIN-ING

The Earl Lectures were established in 1901, and they have included themes important to emerging theologies and practices in ministry. Through more than a century, the Earl Lectures have made critical connections between faith and every day public life. The Pastoral Conference established by the E.T. Earl Foundation consisted of a number of noteworthy leaders in the war years: Rev. Halford Luccock, Adjunct Professor in preaching; Dr. John Coleman Bennet, Professor of Philosophy and Religion; Dr. James Muilenburg, Professor of Old Testament; Dr. John Wright Buckham, Professor Emeritus in Philosophy of Religion; Dr. Chester Carlton McCown, Professor of New Testament; Dr. Arthur Cushman McGiffert, President of Pacific School of Religion. Along with the lectures of Boisen, there were Special Interest Seminars, Faculty Seminars, and worship services. The Conference brochure had educational opportunity.

Under the general title *Crisis and Custom in Religious Experience*, Boisen spoke about three subjects at the Earl Lectures:[238]

1. The Economic Depression and the Rise of the Holy Roller Sects, February 16
2. What War Does to Religion, February 17
3. Religion and the Common Life, February 18 [239]

In preparation for the Earl lectures, he called upon his earlier study of the Holy Rollers and an article he had written entitled "Religion in Hard Times: A Study of the Holy Rollers" that appeared in *Social Action*, published by the Council for Social Action of the Congregational Church and Christian Churches, dated March 15, 1939. It was a series of lectures on sociology of religion. Blankton, the "typical community" was modeled on Bloomington, Indiana. In this study, he used his deep interest in research and his experience as a religious researcher earlier in his life. This long article in *Social Action* is really a *tour-de-force* representing his own theological perspective on the Holiness sects, the Pentecostals, the "Holy Rollers," that informed his perspective on sin and salvation.[240] He also spoke about "What War Does to Religion" that later appeared in an article for the journal *Religion in Life*.

In 1945, Dr. Arthur Cushman McGiffert began a study group that met at "Cush's" home. It included Boisen along with several other prominent individuals in theological education and psychiatry in the Chicago area. McGiffert noted that Boisen, who had begun as a lecturer at Chicago Theological Seminary in 1926, was able to ride the wave of the mood of adventure that was breaking at the University of Chicago.[241]

In the formation of what became the clinical pastoral education movement, Boisen joined the traditional Reformed theological grounding of his youth and early years in the household of his grandfather, with the liberal theology of turn of the century America that was a part of his parent's legacy and certainly the ethos of Union Seminary (NY) when he was a student. He combined the two religious traditions with the pragmatism of William James to emerge with a practical inquiry into theology derived from listening to the variety of religious experiences of individuals and groups. He urged his students to inquire into the lived moments in the day to day experiences of ordinary people that they might discover the elemental questions humankind faces as people try to "be human." There the student will discover the power of doing theology through narrative and personal biography.[242]

His quest was for the "inner genius," that is the attendant religious presence, that drives an individual with the gift of grace, wisdom, love and energy in the face of the ups and downs of daily living. He became an inwardly motivated, quest directed, man. The poignant line of his life developed from within outward, at times dynamically, certainly functionally.

More important, Boisen wanted his students to discover the religious experience that brings people successfully through such struggles. His interest was in the revelation and transformation that emerged out of his own recurring episodes of serious mental illness.[243] Boisen was convinced that "the religious" was the integrating spine, the originating genes of human life. This statement was a bold step forward for theological encounter and discovery.

14

RESEARCH BY CASE STUDY MEETING "LIVING HUMAN DOCUMENTS"

There was a conviction growing out of Boisen's personal experience and his studies in theology, psychology, and the social sciences that theology was *method* as well as content. It was the involvement with "living human documents" that was the indispensable aspect of that method.   It was the approach or method that was new.

Boisen was a research theologian who believed that *method* grounded in the experiential exploration of the life story of individuals and society would bring new understanding of the foundation of religious experience. It could be a way for students, preparing for ministry, to be challenged to think theologically about their encounters, not only with books and theological doctrine, but with "living human documents."   In particular, he saw in mental illness an opportunity to study the function of theological beliefs in periods of crisis.   He was interested in how the beliefs of people impacted their actual life situations. The method of doing this was by research into the life story of individuals and the presentation of comprehensive case histories with theological students and professional colleagues. He was particularly interested in what the person deemed sustaining, guiding and healing in relationship to God, to others, and to the society that nurtured and sustained them, to the community where they could transfer their highest loyalty. This supportive community was what he came to call the "fellowship of the best" with God as representative of what was supreme in the life of the individual and her/his social system of loyalties.[244] Boisen made use of the empirical method he first learned as a forester from Raphael Zon.[245] He had further developed the empirical method in his research in field work with The Reverend Dr. Warren Wilson for the Department of Church and Country Life of the Presbyterian Church Board of Home Missions. Finally, very important was his association with Dr. Richard Cabot at Harvard where he further developed the case study method through involvement in Cabot's class. The title of Cabot's class was, *Preparation for Case Records for Teaching Purposes.*

Dr. Richard Cabot had recognized the value of not only social work in a hospital that he was instrumental in founding in 1905, but also the presence of the minister. One of Cabot's ideas was a clinical year for theological students, as was the common practice of medical students. Cabot lived next to the Episcopal Seminary near Harvard, and he saw students going about their ways on campus. He wondered about the nature of their call to ministry and whether it included learning to work with individuals who were in trouble of mind, body, and soul. Early in the movement, Boisen and others considered Dr. Richard Cabot the originator of the case method in medical education and in theological education as well.

Traditionally, ministers had been admonished by the way of lectures and study of texts on pastoral ministry, to *do* "this or that" for people in need. Read scripture, pray prescribed prayers from the book of prayers, offer sacraments, and tell the patient what he or she needed for religious nurturing. An empiricist like Boisen drew rules of practice not from theory or admonition by lecture, but from close observation and experiment, emphasizing the inductive method rather than the deductive method of learning. The basic idea behind empiricism was that knowledge can be derived through careful observation and cataloging of phenomena and extrapolating principles from these observations. Boisen used the study of the preparation of case records for teaching purposes and the Clinical Pathological Conferences of Cabot to develop a methodology that became his most important contribution in theological education.[246]

Empiricism denies that humans have innate ideas or that anything is knowable prior to experience. In contrast, Rationalists claim that there are significant ways in which concepts and knowledge are gained independent of sense experience. Empiricists, however, claim that sense experience is the ultimate source of all concepts and knowledge.[247]

As a critique, Boisen felt that the empirical method was lacking in the liberal theology of his time. The Reverend Dr. Allison Stokes, in her book *Ministry after Freud*, points out that Boisen had made an extensive survey of the liberal theological literature and found it deficient in the empirical method. "In doing theology empirically, he followed the revelation of his own experience and studied the experiences of the mentally ill. He found in the people he studied a belief in the revelatory power of experience."[248]

Dr. Robert C. Powell wrote that Boisen was well aware that he was "leading a revolution in theological education." What was involved was a thoroughgoing shift of attention and a new method of attack and in the end a new authority for the clergy, grounded not in tradition, nor theological dogma, but in human experience.

That shift from books to the nitty-gritty world had something compelling about it, sparked by a patient turned clinician on behalf of suffering patients.

Boisen had discovered William James back in Bloomington, and James called his philosophy *radical empiricism*. James wrote: "Ideas become true just in so far as they help us to get into satisfactory relation with other parts of our experience, to summarize them and get about, among them, by conceptual short-cuts instead of following interminable successions of particular phenomena."[249]

Harvard Professor Dr. Charles Sanders Peirce, in a January 1878 article, "How to Make Our Ideas Clear," published in *Popular Science Monthly*, wrote that "our beliefs are really *rules for action*. To develop a thought's meaning, we need only determine what conduct it is fitted to produce, that conduct is for us its sole significance. To attain perfect clearness in our thoughts of an object, then, we need only consider what conceivable *effects of a fractal[250] kind the object may involve*, what sensations we are to expect form it, [what outcome is to be expected] and what reactions we must prepare."[251]

Professor Peirce, along with John Dewey and William James, were recognized as the founders of the philosophical school of American Pragmatism. All three were leading agents of the Progressive Movement in American education during the early years of Boisen's life. The Pragmatist turns away from abstraction and insufficiency, from verbal solutions, from bad *a priori* reasons, from fixed principles, closed systems, and pretended absolutes and origins. The Pragmatist turns toward concreteness and adequacy, towards facts, towards action. It means the open air and the possibilities of nature, as against dogma, artificiality, and the pretence of finality in truth-telling.

Boisen remembered that William James taught that impressions arose out of the necessity of organizing the often confused facts of experience. James began to address this particular phenomenon as he tried to keep his head above water during a period of depression, or "stagnation" as he called it. The value of concepts was not absolute but relative to their practical consequences. The empirical method interprets each concept by tracing its practical consequences, its uses.

Most theologies proceed by reflection on what *is* the general character of things, "a priori" knowledge, [252]and deductive knowledge. "In general," wrote Boisen, "we have not gone on to base theological study upon the sources of all understanding of human nature, that being the first hand observation of human experience, both in individuals and in their social relationships."[253] Empirical theology begins with a *particular* situation. It is this *particular* that distinguishes the empirical theologian from the rationalistic theologian whose thinking is based on theory and doctrine rather than on experience. William James wrote in another context about radical empiricism: "I am interested in radical empiricism, and it seems to me that the establishment of the pragmatist theory[254] of truth are steps of first rate importance in making radical empiricism prevail. Radical empiricism consists first of a postulate, next of a statement of fact, and finally of a generalized conclusion."

The *postulate* is that the only things that shall be debatable among philosophers shall be things definable in terms drawn from experience.

The *statement of fact* is that the relations between things are matters of direct particular experience.

The *generalized conclusion* is that therefore the parts of experience hold from next to next by relations that are themselves parts of experience.[255]

In radical empiricism, the flux of perceived experience is primary. The theory of radical empiricism is the most original and fruitful contribution to philosophy by William James.[256] Professor Brooks Holifield wrote: "Boisen had admired William James because of his perspective on the 'sick soul' and not because of his doctrine of the will. Boisen had criticized the liberal psychology of religion because of its optimism about human nature."

Boisen had enrolled in Dr. Cabot's Harvard University course on *Preparation for Case Records for Teaching Purposes.* He looked back upon it and said that it was one of the best courses he had ever taken.[257] From Cabot he became familiar with the case study method and recognized its power as a part of the learning process. It was basically this method that he introduced with the student group that came to Worcester the summer of 1925. The case study method was Boisen's principal training tool.

Boisen believed that the very first quality for theological education was that it should stimulate thinking theologically for the student. It was not the intention of Boisen to steer a student into any given theology, but to encourage the student to use his/her own theological heritage in the practical field. The foundation of authority was the sacred perspective of the religious experience, and thinking theologically was grounded in the empirical study of the phenomena of religious experience.

"Boisen had a diversity of theological views and interests," commented Hiltner.[258] He believed throughout his career, that empirical inquiry into religious experience would help correct the excessive individualism in American Protestantism. Boisen was not only interested in individuals but *also individuals in community, in society.* Boisen's method was gained from scientific observation. He placed the outcome of the observation into a theological context. Traditional theological categories are called upon, e.g. sin and salvation, conversion, redemption, the fellowship of the best, but they are called upon in the context of living human interaction.

With the same zeal, Boisen disapproved of students who did not supplement their clinical learning by reading to make an informed interpretation and statement. Boisen's method of doing theology forced students to make an *informed interpretation* of the experiences they heard the patients tell and that they recorded in their own case studies. Real learning takes place within the creative interplay of experience and concept.

Boisen's case studies involved in-depth interviews with a patient, often over an extended time period, sometimes years. They included a detailed review of the patient's life situation and analysis of the gathered information about the patient. Boisen used mainly case studies of people with various mental illnesses. Boisen showed his ability to communicate with the patient in her or his often twisted world.

In 1927, while Boisen was a chaplain at Worcester State Hospital, Dr. R. G. Hoskins, of Harvard Medical School, an endocrinologist, was studying 173 patients considering the ethical and religious factors, as well as the medical diagnosis, primarily Dementia Praecox.[259] The research team concluded that whatever the organic basis for Dementia Praecox, for the sufferer it is primarily an experience beyond the physiological dimension. Boisen was given the freedom to study the same patients from his own perspective. Boisen's study shows that moral self judgment is among the most important causative factors in the mental illness of the patients.

He wrote about the cases: "The examination of the causative factors in Dementia Praecox has led us to the conclusion that the primary evil lies in the realm of social relationships, particularly in a life situation involving the sense of personal failure. We have found one characteristic common to the group as a whole: they are isolated from their fellows through a social judgment that either consciously or subconsciously they accept and pronounce upon themselves."[260]

He listed three important factors as being the motivation and response to conflict, a sense of personal failure, and distress: "Drifting, Self Deception, and Panic."

Drifting: Several of these individuals made little or no resistance. They did not fight, or attempt to turnover a new leaf. They did not try to do anything about their condition. They took refuge in the easy modes of satisfaction. The drive for self-realization was short circuited and the person became more listless and ineffective and unable to take care of him/herself. He/she became a burden on family, healthcare facilities, and the state.

Self Deception and delusional misrepresentation: There were many others who in the face of threatening failure refused to admit defeat or error and resorted to distortion of belief. Most of the beliefs came out of their own life situation and represented attempts to meet the stresses of existence. Most of the beliefs were incorrect, but the delusional misinterpretations of the psychotic type are carried out in an extreme mode so that the individual is isolated from the group.

Panic: Few can drift down to destruction or succeed in building up an effective system of delusional misinterpretation without at some time becoming aware of the danger. This will result in a greater or lesser form of emotional disturbance that may appear as profound despair and hopelessness in which the patient loses all interest in the external world. It also may occur as an acute upheaval This was not regarded as evil, but was analogous to attempt at a cure, signaled by fever and inflammation in the physical body

The religious concerns most often appeared whenever individuals were facing difficulty and were dealing with ultimate values.[261]   Boisen came to the conclusion, early in his career at Worcester State Hospital, that patients are often engaged in problem solving experiences that are closely related to individual types of religious experience. There was a significant likeness to a religious conversion experience. It was typical for those who had a tendency for the panic reaction to produce change either for the better or for the worse. It was on this conclusion that Boisen built his further research in the theological dimension as he observed living human beings. These cases were the foundation and source for theological understanding.

In support of his perspective on the experiential aspects of Dementia Praecox, he cited the case of Albert W in whom he found "a baseline for the examination of the inner meaning of the schizophrenic experience." This summary is from a copy of Albert W's case study by Boisen in "The Experiential Aspects of Dementia Praecox," in the *American Journal of Psychiatry*, Vol. XIII, No 3, and November 1933.

Albert W.

Albert W. was a migrant worker with the intelligence of the seventh grader. He had had about all the handicaps a boy might have in the matter of heredity and early childhood influences. His parents and grandfather had been heavy drinkers. The parents were committed to the state institution with alcohol problems. He was persistently disobedient, dishonest, untruthful, and quarrelsome. As an adult he had not been able to hold a job very long. Gambling and women accounted for a good portion of his spent earnings. He started masturbation at fourteen and had his first heterosexual experience at fifteen.   In reform school, he had participated in homosexual activity with the boys. He did have a serious love affair with the sister of his brother-in-law. The termination of this affair left him deeply depressed.

A couple of months before admission to the hospital, he felt something strange going on. He believed charges were being lodged against him. He went to the police. He was dismissed and continued wanderings, becoming more and more disturbed. He became overwhelmed with fear of the unknown. Communications came from "out of the ether." First Jonah, then St. Augustine, then Christ, then the solar system appeared. He felt that he was in Paradise. He took trips beyond the confines of earth. He was admitted to hospital.

At the hospital, after the disturbance abated, he made a good adjustment. He left the hospital, and he was cooperative and dependable. The disturbance was for him a religious experience, something that had given him new life and new hope.

The final outcome was not so good, however, for he had a relapse and when Boisen returned from a three month absence, he found him disturbed and antagonistic. Boisen then commented, "The case is thoroughly representative of the acutely disturbed type in which the outcome is most apt to be favorable."[262] Throughout his first hospitalization he was concerned about life and death, survival and destruction, and his relationship to the universe that supported and sustained him. Then he was translated into heaven. He visualized himself passing from an earthly to a higher realm, from red to white, and he felt that he had been touched within by the Holy Grail. His was a profound religious awakening and experience. From the disturbed period, he emerged with the feeling that he had passed from an earthly existence into the spiritual life.[263]

In reviewing this, and other cases, Boisen was not so much interested in *doing something for* the mental patient as much as *learning about* the patient, and whether that patient is moving on a positive or a negative path toward healing as shown in the case of Albert W. He would include in his studies a number of graphs and charts showing what one could learn from the case about religious concern according to the Reaction Patterns of the patients. The act of entering into the life of a patient, asking her or him questions in a research mode, being there and paying attention, can have benefits for the individual in making adjustment to their life situation. He analyzed the religious ideation of patients, as well as their reaction patterns.

When Boisen began his program at Worcester State Hospital in 1925, he used for his seminary students a model that was guided by the method in depth he learned under Raphael Zon as a forester; and Dr. Richard Cabot's model that he learned in his "Social Ethics Seminar on Case Records for Teaching Purposes" at Harvard University in 1922 and 1923.

Dr. Cabot had developed what he titled "The Essentials of Case Records for Teaching Purposes." The essentials included.

(1. The preliminary orientation and statement of the problem.
(2. Is there an adequate picture of the personality and situation?
(3. Is there an adequate analysis of the facts for judgment and action?"

Dr. Cabot listed 36 items for the "Essentials of Case Records."[264] To this was attached a definition of "Psychiatric Terms and Concepts." Cabot utilized the case study method in his Clinical Pathological Conferences at Harvard.

In an article published much later, in 1959, in *The Journal of Pastoral Care*, titled "Religious Experience and Psychological Conflict,"

Boisen summarized the basic theory about religion and mental illness that had guided his case study method from the beginning: "There are forms of mental illness which are manifestations of healing power analogous to fever or inflammation of the body. These are the forms of mental disorder in which, as chaplain in a mental hospital, I have been especially interested. There are periods in the development of the personality when the individual feels himself face to face with ultimate Reality, periods in which fate hangs in the balance. In such periods, religious concern is much in evidence and the creative forces are exceptionally active. So just as well are forms of destruction. There are periods of seething emotion that tend either to make or break. As such they are closely related to the dramatic conversion experience which has been so prominent in the history of the Christian church since the days of Saul of Tarsus."[265]

Dr. Glenn Asquith, Jr. stated that Anton Boisen had a two-fold objective for his case study method. He was both interested in the individual experience as well as a study of the experience of people in society. Boisen said, "I have sought to begin not with the ready-made formulations contained in books, but with the living human document, and with actual social conditions in all their complexity."[266] His study of actual social conditions was well sharpened from his early experience with social survey and study of rural church communities in conjunction with his friend, Fred Eastman, under the direction of Rev. Dr. Warren Wilson for the Presbyterian Church.

Boisen had two goals for his case study method.

First, his interest was in the development of the case method as research into the relationship between theology and the psychology of religious experience;

Second, his interest was to stimulate the theological thinking of seminary students about lived human experience.

He began to develop the case study method while still a patient at Westboro State Hospital. Using those case studies, along with a number of others, he challenged the student to get in touch with his/her own religious and theological heritage through discussion of the case being presented. He wanted the student to start with the lived human encounter with the patient, and then draw out of the experience his/her own theological belief. His interest was in disciplined theological reflection on what the student encountered in the case study regarding the patient and the patient's social groups and environment. To accomplish this, he would attach to each case a set of four or five questions to guide the student into theological thinking. He was interested in focusing on the religious meaning of the patient's experience.[267] For a number of years, Boisen used the pre-prepared case studies of patients for the seminary student to read and reflect when they would meet for class.

Two more cases illustrate his method. Both of these cases are in the *Boisen Collection* at Chicago Theological Seminary, Hammond Library, file cabinet 2, and drawer titled "Mimeographed Records – Hospital cases."

Jonah

First, there is the case of *Jonah*. I personally found this story of Ben Mickle, "the Prophet *Jonah*," to be of profound interest. Ben was a simple, straight-forward, no nonsense, what's for dinner kind of guy who was in touch with both his anger and his gentleness. He was a man with a lot of courage, "I never moan or cry." When he "got a mad on" he would fight like a tiger, hurling pots and whatever he could get his hands on with reckless abandon. He could not believe that the Man-Above would have given him two good fists if He had not meant him to use them in fighting. It was the fighting that kept him in the hospital.

He had a mental age of eight years on the Stanford-Binet Psychometric Examination. He was a deeply disturbed man who wrestled with God and the angels until he was led out of the valley of darkness into the light of his call to ministry, a unique ministry to the people of Nineveh that would bring in the Kingdom of God. In the course of time, he had made a 3,200 mile trip to try and find Nineveh.

He belonged to the Missionary Baptist Church. His was a tiny universe, limited to himself and the Man-Above. He believed that the Man-Above had a plan for him and the Man-Above was in full control. "What held him back was that he dealt with life by a reliance on force. He was particularly concerned with his "signals" and "with the mystical identification so closely associated with the signals as a matter of special interest in the interrelationship of religious experience and mental disorder." Boisen comments further, "As to the signals, the mediaeval mystics had to learn the lesson that some of the ideas which came surging into their minds could hardly come from God. They assumed that they must come from the devil. Perhaps we of today need to learn the converse lesson, that all auditory hallucinations do not necessarily come from the devil but may represent the operations of the creative mind."[268]

Ben Mickle felt he had a special channel of communication with the Man Above. Ben had a deep religious sensitivity, and his relationship with the Man Above was a great strength to him. It enabled him to endure great suffering, gave him a structure for his life, solidity, a depth, which he otherwise would not have had.

He did have the problem of using his fists too freely, but so far as Boisen could tell, this was the only serious psychological difficulty he had. The patient was not released from the mental hospital partly because the psychiatrist was concerned that he continued to communicate with the Man Above

Throughout his ministry in the mental hospital, Boisen was keenly interested in the "voices" and "signals" and what they meant to the patient. Ben Mickle compares very favorably with others, like George Fox and John Bunyan, when it came to signals and other openings. His was a single-hearted devotion to an ideal. In a traditional religious context his "signals" were not dissimilar from "inspiration" or "verbal automatism." It was common to poets, inventors, creative individuals. Boisen's Union Seminary professor George Coe believed they were the primitive root of all mystical experience.[269]

Boisen recognized the man or woman who is putting up a struggle against odds for the attainment of some semblance of a "good life." Ben was engaged in a desperate conflict. It was of significance that there was in these cases a religious idea, namely, where the patient attempts to face his or her difficulties and discover some means of change there was found religious ideas. Religion as a resource and strength came through confession and forgiveness,

Boisen stayed with him during good times and bad times, over several years, showing forth his interest in this man's story and demonstrating his perseverance to be-with and to be for-him. Boisen wrote of Mickle: "For me, Mickle always seemed a work of art or, better perhaps, an artist himself. I have found no little enjoyment in some of his shrewd observations and quaint phrases." [270]

Boisen listed several references for the student to read in considering the case of Ben Mickle, titled *Jonas*. He recommended consideration of George Bernard Shaw's *Saint Joan*, pp. 17-27;

ANTON THEOPHILUS BOISEN:

George A. Coe's *A Psychology of Religion*, Chapters 11, 12, 16; E.D. Hutchinson's "Insight in Relation to Religion," *Psychiatry*, 6 (1943) pp 347-357; Campbell's *Delusion and Belief*, and his own *Exploration of the Inner World, A Study of Mental Disorder and Religious Experience*, p.312.

According to Boisen, sexual difficulty figured predominantly in most of the cases in the hospital. It usually represented something one was afraid to talk about and therefore gave rise to a sense of guilt. Many of his case studies involved some sexual situation that was not working well for the patient. The Reverend Clarence Bruninga, a former student, said that he presented case studies to his students, many of which had problems of sex involving the patient, family member, girl and boy friend. The selection of case study material reflected as much on Boisen's personhood as on the patient. [271] He regularly forced much through the sieve of his own experience.

Don Juan

To illustrate a case coming from the Worcester period the story of "John P, the Penitent Don Juan" was a 38-year-old brick mason fearful of what might happen to his wife.[272] This was a case of severe anxiety due to an uneasy conscience. He was an illegitimate child adopted by kindly foster parents who died when he was 12 years of age. He was then brought up by a relative of the foster parent. His chief problem seemed to lie in the sexual sphere, having had numerous sexual relations with prostitutes throughout his life followed by several more permanent relationships with an unfortunate outcome in one instance, there having been an abortion involved. Sex love, for Boisen at its best, approached religion. In the case study of John P., Boisen has chosen a patient with sexual problems similar to his own.

Sex was uppermost in the mind of John P. This began when he was 15 years old. Boisen considered this maladjustment. Experimentations and so on, to which this man was addicted, was standing in the way of finer relationships that should have been possible later on. What brought on his disturbance was the increasing uneasiness that arose out of his early sexual life. The thing most on his mind was the breach of loyalty toward the woman who had taken the place of a mother in his own feelings. The disturbance came following the death of this woman, and he blamed himself for that. After having been admitted to hospital, symptoms got worse. He was in a strange and mysterious universe, and things were not as they seemed. All went purple in color Likewise, the number five which appeared ominous cropped up several times during a given day. There were also rules, rules, and rules. He had not lived up to the rule of common society.

John P had been a social drinker, until the period of his sexual maladjustment. He stopped drinking, and then made confession to his wife to tell her about his previous relationships. The important thing was to get rid of the fear of telling. He was committed to hospital, and then "he got well." He got along nicely and became a successful contractor.

Boisen said that the anxiety and guilt that John P experienced was a hopeful and positive prognosis in this case. If he ceased to be anxious, his prognosis would have been unhappy. His anxiety and guilt, confessed, and accepted, resulted in something that was wholesome. There was a transfer of loyalty from the finite to the infinite.

In a mimeographed document, "Types of Mental Illness: A Beginning Course for the Use in Training Centers for the Council for Clinical Training of Theological Students," Boisen's research interests were made clear: He wrote, "This course is far less concerned with the consideration of techniques and skills than with the effort to discover the forces involved in the spiritual life and the laws by which they operate. It seeks to lay a foundation for the co-operative attempt to organize and test religious experience and to build a theology on the basis of a careful scrutiny of religious beliefs."[273]

Student Responsibilities

The term for a summer unit of training was usually June through Labor Day. The program was:

1. Frequent group conferences with the assistance of members of the Medical Staff for the consideration of theological implications
2. Practical contribution to the welfare of patients,
3. Supervised case study work,
4. Staff meetings - expected to attend

The student was expected to write daily observations plus one or two intensive case studies during the CPE unit. The student was to provide ministry to the patient, not to lecture or probe, and to befriend the patient, while keeping eyes and ears open for questions and responses to show the student's interest in order to draw the patient out. It was an opportunity to serve and to observe.[274]

Students also had responsibility for the hospital's weekly news-sheet, *The Messenger,* trying to make it something really worth while to read. They made an annual Hospital Pictorial of events and writings, which included pictures, poetry, and prose stories about individuals within the hospital community.[275] The students would sometimes direct a play and present it for the nurses at the time of graduation. The students helped with the regular worship services. Boisen had designed the worship service to meet the special needs of the hospital community. The reading and prayers and hymns were selected by Boisen for the special needs of "those passing through the valley of conflict and shadow."[276] Besides this kind of activity, the students were expected to do efficient work on the wards and do a penetrating study of the cases assigned to them.

What I have noted in reading the case histories is that Boisen does little or no defining of the theological themes himself. He thoroughly describes the history of the patient, leaving the form theological reflection would take to the student's discretion. He expected the student to do this work out of the context of his or her own religious background. By this means, Boisen avoided imposing strongly his own theology before the student had her or his chance to voice an opinion, drawing on their own religious tradition. A case analysis would consist of the following details.

Physical findings
1. Psychological testing
2. Social and religious background
3. Personal history
    a. Childhood
    b. School years
    c. Adolescence and Maturity
    d. Sex Code
    e. Religion and faith background

Attitude toward same and toward opposite sex
1. Love affairs and disappointment
2. Marriage
3. Vocational adjustments

ANTON THEOPHILUS BOISEN:

Diagnostics

1. Physical condition and health
2. Present illness
3. Characteristics of the disorder
4. Present condition
5. Religious attitude and orientation here and now
6. Diagnostic impression

Observation, progress notes and interpretation

He defined his teaching method in a letter to the Executive Director of the Council for Clinical Training, Fred Kuether, dated 21 September 1954. This statement is at the heart of Boisen's concept of soul-care (*Seelsorge*).[277] "From the beginning of this undertaking, it has been my constant claim that we were not seeking to introduce anything into the already over-crowded curriculum of the theological schools. We have instead been trying to call attention back to the age-old problem of sin, of salvation, of prophetic inspiration. What is new is the approach. In a time when students of religion have been making little use of the methods of science, and the humanistic scientists have failed to carry their inquiries to the level of the religious, we have been making empirical studies of the living human documents, particularly those in which men [and women] are breaking or have broken under the strain of moral crises."[278]

Seward Hiltner commented that Boisen attempted, with remarkable success, to bring the results of science and religion together in an integrated way. The Fundamentalists in America at this time saw religion as being against science. I believe that Boisen would say something like this: "Medicine is the most scientific of the humanities and most humane of the sciences."

If we consider pastoral care to embody *Seelsorge*, then the "primary task of pastoral care is to tend to the soul,"[279] it is a ministry of the care (or cure) of souls. Pastoral care is rightly understood as *Seelsorge* or companioning the soul on its journey to God. Pastoral care consists of useful acts, done by *caring people*. Herbert Anderson writes in an article, "Whatever Happened to *Seelsorge?*": "Although pastoral care has fostered careful listening to human stories, it has not attended equally well to the stories of God. Recovery of the care of souls (*Seelsorge*) can help build bridges between the human and the divine."[280]

From the files at Chicago Theological Seminary, *Boisen Collection*, I have chosen, at random, thirty five (35) cases, from both Worcester State Hospital in Massachusetts and Elgin State Hospital in Illinois. There are some general characteristics of these cases.

The religious connection of the patients tended to be with young churches, the Christian and Missionary Alliance, the Holy Rollers evangelists such as Billy Sunday or Dwight L. Moody, and other religious groups mainly in opposition to the scientific concept of Darwinian evolution. Only a few were associated with the main-line churches: Lutheran, Baptist, Presbyterian, and Roman Catholic.

Many of the individuals had very negative sexual adjustments to life, either through promiscuity or through long periods of masturbation from an early age for which there is associated a sense of guilt. Of the number of cases read, only four or five did not have any major sexual maladjustment. This may very well reflect Boisen's own subjective selectivity toward an interest in sexual maladjustment.

Other presenting problems included the following

1. Excessive drinking and marital conflict
2. Anxiety reaction carried to the point of severe psychosis

3. Sense of guilt and isolation

Oscar O put to test of giving up his life for a wife he increasingly disliked

One case entitled, "A Page of the Blessed Virgin," is a case in which he and Dr. Jules Masserman, at Elgin State Hospital, had differing interpretations. Boisen's interpretation was a good illustration of his basic hypothesis about religious experience and schizophrenia. The story goes like this:

Dr. Masserman was a prominent Chicago psychiatrist and Elgin Consultant who viewed the patient at Elgin Sate Hospital as a "classic example of a schizophrenic process." The patient went into a schizophrenic tail spin when her manipulative structure in real life broke down, when her foster father, her lawyer and her minister forsook her. Her fantasy and wishful thinking continued. She conceived of herself as a "page of the Blessed Virgin" – a high and important role of which she was the center. The Judge was God and God was on her side. She was a female Jesus. Hers was a universal fantasy of a Last Judgment Day because it was necessary for the draining off of anxiety. There are a number of individuals who in the face of accumulating difficulties withdrew into the realm of fantasy and wishful thinking. So in Dr. Masseerman's view, the patient had not learned a lesson and it was not to be expected that she would make an improved adjustment after she left the hospital.

Boisen, on the other hand, saw her in a hopeful light as a bright, attractive girl of superior intelligence, brought up in a well-to-do family of a foster father in which schizophrenic thinking became a creative process. This woman had had, however, an extremely unsatisfactory life characterized by light-hearted irresponsibility. Boisen's analysis followed.

1. Even if light-hearted, she had been out-going and friendly.

There was a deeper side to her nature represented by her "Bible reading, prayer and keeping a diary." The disturbance followed a momentous event, the birth of a baby causing her to think about what mattered most. She had done something virtuous and sacrificial, the father of the baby had offered to marry her, but she refused because she could not see a marriage based on a mistake. The disturbance began with prayer, Bible reading, intense pre-occupation and sleeplessness compromising her judgment and perspective. She tried to work out a valid philosophy of life, who am I, what am I meant to be and do? What is my relationship with God?

2. Her case ran a continuum extending from acute and destructive mental disorder to religious experience in its more dramatic manifestation. Her disturbance was a manifestation of the power to heal analogous to fever or inflammation in the body. The therapist needed to recognize the meaning of such experiences and work with the healing forces and not against them. Hope of a constructive outcome depended on helping the girl to believe in herself and to believe in this experience as something more than just a nervous break-down.

Failure to recognize the religious significance of such a case as this was something far deeper than a matter of semantics. It was analogous to the failure to recognize that the earth goes round the sun instead of the sun round the earth. It meant failure to understand mental disorder in its wider implications and failure to make the contribution that psychiatry ought to make toward the understanding of human nature either individually or collectively. While his statistical base was slender, figures do suggest that schizophrenic reactions tended either to make or break the patient or to produce change either for better or for worse.[281] He would consistently ask the student in the CPE program as they reviewed cases: "Is it possible to have mental disorder and religious experience in one and the same person at the same time?"

During 1946 and 1947, the students got involved in an extended study of 75 admission cases that they reported on during a summer unit; Boisen reported this in an article, "The Onset of Acute Schizophrenia," published in *Psychiatry*, May 1947. Fifty-four of these patients felt that they were in direct contact with the superhuman. "More than half engaged in prayer and Bible-reading. Twenty six were overwhelmed with remorse for past sins. All of them, during the acute phase of the disturbance, were grappling with the central problem of theology and philosophy as with matters of life and death." It was evident from this study that the psychiatrist needed to have some sense of the religious factor in the lives of the patients and needed to help them to interpret the experience and to see it in true perspective.

Boisen wrote in another context of a number of men and women of unquestioned religious genius who have passed through Schizophrenic or Schizoaffective episodes in the process of finding themselves. The list is impressive: John Bunyan, George Fox, David Brainerd, Heinrich Suso, Emanual Swedenborg, Søren Kierkegaard, Saint Teresa, and Paul of Tarsus. Boisen's studies of them are mainly composed of quotations from the writings of each individual and comments about the life of each person. There is an emphasis upon their conversion experience and how that changed the direction of their lives. Boisen was interested in Fox, Bunyan, Brainerd, and the others because he felt that they had had experiences similar to those seen in the mental hospital.

He not only had class and study for seminary students; in 1941, he developed a curriculum for pastors in congregations. He called it, "Problems in Religion and Life for Pastors." He wrote an extensive syllabus and outlined a survey method for the clergy to use locally in their congregations. The focus of the teaching for pastors was on the mentally ill as Boisen felt that the church had done very little for these individuals. The following is a brief summary of the main points in his material for pastor.

He defined various mental illnesses: Psychosis, Psycho-neurosis, Epilipsy, Psychopathic disturbances. Mental illness included the alcoholic, the delinquent person, the sexually maladjusted, and the physically ill. He asked three basic questions for the use by pastors in ministering to the mentally ill:

1. When was the beginning of the disturbance?
2. What are the causative factors present?
3. What is the present picture?

The principles of personal pastoral counseling included:

1. Religious conversion experience
2. Religion of under privileged
3. Religion and Social Action
4. Religious education
5. Distinctive task of the minister of religion[282]

As the Clinical Pastoral Education movement grew toward its present form, the verbatim record of a pastoral care interview was adopted in most centers. This was instituted by The Reverend Russell Dicks at Massachusetts General Hospital. The verbatim form fit better with the type of pastoral visits made in a general hospital. This development was a disappointment to Boisen.

Dr. Cushman McGiffert, Jr., a colleague with Boisen at Chicago Theological Seminary, remembered him vividly when interviewed

60 years later.[283]   One of Anton Boisen's significant contributions was that "he could learn from other fields and others could learn from him." He and McGiffert taught a course together entitled "Experience and Theology." This course began with hospital experience and went on from those cases of recognized religious experience as they tried to reach generalizations that might be related to the historical doctrines of the church "regarding sin and salvation, to regeneration and sanctification, to inspiration and belief."[284] Co-teaching in theological education was rare at this time. Boisen helped lead the way by participating in this multidisciplinary teaching.

In teaching this course he wanted to show the fact that he felt that the main importance of the experience at the hospital was in the light that it may throw upon the laws that pertain to the care of the soul with which theology is concerned and thus in its bearing upon the church's message of warning and hope. His desire was to "map the little known country of the inner world in order that those still in the land of the living may be saved from falling into the abyss in which we labor and may be led in safety to their Promised Land."[285]

A religious discussion group that met at Dr. McGiffert's home, worked together. There would be a sociologist, an ethicist, a theologian, a social worker, and Boisen; and this had a lot to do with breaking down the disciplinary divisions. The five met to present cases. At these informal meetings, McGiffert said: "Boisen was wonderful at writing up cases. He had it going in academia, but he still had difficulty with the informal social settings." One of his remarkable contributions was that he could gather from other fields and others could be trained from an encounter with him. Boisen helped lead the way by participating in this multidisciplinary teaching.

Dr. McGiffert said that "he would bring a psychiatrist from the downtown Chicago Loop to be with the student group.

Boisen was curious about others and eager to see what light they might shed on the problem he had worked on all of his life. He worked along two different lines: (1) the subject itself. (2) the interdisciplinary approach."[286] He was adept at involving others in an interdisciplinary approach and breaking down disciplinary fences in the academic world. Boisen made a noteworthy contribution to theological education by his passion for the scientific method and the adaptation of the case study model of clinical research to theological education. Boisen wanted theological students to pay attention to experiences they encountered in pastoral conversations in order to integrate theology with scientific research methods. Boisen had written early in his career at Worcester State Hospital "A Challenge to our Seminaries."[287]

The student was challenged to build a body of theological knowledge from lived experiences using the case study method for research. Boisen's method expected students to give an informed interpretation of the experiences they reported and discussed. He showed that there was a creative interplay between internationality and surprise.

There was a National Conference sponsored by the Council for Clinical Training held at Western Theological Seminary in 1944. Seward Hiltner gave a lecture on the development of the Clinical Training Movement. At the conclusion there was an open discussion. Russell Dicks asked Boisen, who was present, whether his primary purpose was to bring relief to sick people or to train ministers? Boisen replied that his primary interest had been educational, but that the therapeutic interest had also been prominent. In Boisen there was an informed, sound theological intention in learning, and at the same time there was openness to the unexpected, the new astonishment.

15

THE THEOLOGICAL LEGACY OF ANTON BOISEN

Anton Boisen was first of all a research-oriented theologian. He thought individuals best learned by listening and observing as they offered caring acts. He maintained a theological perspective regarding psychology and the social sciences, the instruction about humanity. His goal was not to construct a system of belief. His task was to organize and test the effect of religion on the story of human experience as a way of learning about the influence and meaning of beliefs about God, suffering and sin, confession and conversion, salvation and regeneration. He wanted to validate the care of the soul in and through the religious community, what Boisen called the Fellowship of the Best.[288] Theology was the study of religious belief and the dynamic forces in the lives of individuals, rather than a statement of belief itself.[289] When asked about God, Boisen said he believed in a supreme being that he called *The Idea of God*.

For Boisen, research was aimed at confirming, or disavowing, ideas about the relationship of religious experience and mental illness. Initially, the branch of theology known as pastoral theology came out of reflection upon ministry with people in need. Boisen did not intend his method to necessarily help the student in his personal psychological formation. Boisen depended on the student to be mature enough to do that on her own. He would provide a good resource if the student wanted it and asked for it. The challenge was for the student to understand the theology of her own religious community as it was experienced in the care-giving relationship with another. The confrontation to the student was to encourage theological reflection. He wanted students to learn to think theologically from conversation with the person in need and with supervised reflection upon that encounter.

Boisen defined theology "as the attempt, either individually or collectively, to organize and scrutinize the beliefs regarding, the end and meaning of life, the spiritual forces that operate within us, and, the relationships which exist between their various manifestations, all in the light of the belief in a supreme reality to whom men generally give the name God." He continued, "From ethics and philosophy, theology is distinguished by the fact that it is concerned with the realm of religious experience and belief; whereas ethics is concerned with interpersonal relations and values without reference to the faith in a super-personal Being; and philosophy is the attempt to organize and interpret all of human experience."[290] Theology dealt with the internalization of thoughts and feelings about God.[291]

Boisen wrote "as individuals come face to face with the ultimate realities of life and death, religion and theology tend to come alive. Theology has always been concerned with the motivating beliefs of men regarding their origin and destiny and their relationship to the universe. It has dealt with what is supreme in the hierarchy of desires and values and with the choices that favor or impede maximum self realization."[292] He based this theory on research with a "limited number of people, most of whom had passed through periods of crisis with radical changes in personality, some for the better, and some for the worse."

For Boisen, the central focus of his theology was exploring the spiritual nature of the other by an exploration of his own inner struggles. He believed that even when human conflict escalated to schizophrenic intensity, it could be liberating. Jesus and St. Paul, as they faced conflict, were liberated from immutable destruction. His favorite Biblical text was John 3:16. "God so loved the world that he gave his only son, so that everyone who believes in Him may not be lost, but may have eternal life." (*Jerusalem Bible* published in the USA in1968)[293] He was concerned that the daily problems of his existence directly impacted the development of his perspective on the nature of the human condition. This came from his struggles as a psychiatric patient, as well as listening to the stories of psychiatric patients, along with his own extensive reading in the social and psychological sciences. It was this pragmatic approach – gathering evidence of human *existence* and using it to derive the *essence* of the religious experience of the divine – that made Boisen's method distinctive.

For Boisen, human individuality lay in the realm of soul care (*cura animarum*). It was life under God and for God's glory. Boisen was, on the one hand, decisive in his approach. He meticulously explored the boundary of another's story; and on the other hand, he made one feel at ease by the graciousness of his gentle manner. Father Henri J. M. Nouwen said, "He was a man who lived out his ministry focused on the love of God, and usefulness to all of humanity."[294] Len Cedarleaf wrote about an interview in 1943. He was "startled by his Episcopal appearance and age (67) but he quickly made me feel at ease."[295]

ANTON THEOPHILUS BOISEN:

Boisen's Theological Legacy

First, his legacy was that he believed clinical pastoral education was an integral part of theological education. It was not on the psychiatric or psychological periphery. For him, theology was the "Queen of the Sciences." The entire seventh chapter of Boisen's *Exploration of the Inner World: A Study of Mental Disorder and Religious Experience* is devoted to the "Queen of the Sciences."[296] He believed that theology deserved a place among the sciences.

As pointed out earlier, Boisen's theology was informed by the union of two major influences.

First, there was the Scotch-Irish Covenanter Presbyterianism of his grandfather's home that ran throughout his long life. The faith was critically-oriented and intellectually alert with a strong sentiment of morality and piety. There was the importance of the Providence of God. It was God showing care for all of creation. In principle, the Covenanter Presbyterian followed the Scottish *Solemn League and Covenant* and the *Westminster Confession of Faith* of 1643.

Second, there was the progressive open-minded influence of his mother and the memory of his father with a hearty dose of the theological liberalism of the early 20th century. He was also influenced by Professors George Albert Coe and William Adams Brown at Union Theological Seminary, two of the foremost theologians of liberal theology.

A **second** legacy was that Boisen set a middle course informed by both traditions. First, he was defined by the household of his grandparents, even as he sought his way out of it. The identity developed in the early years became the lens through which other relations were viewed later in life. Second, both parents were more progressive in their religious life than was Grandfather Wylie. His mother especially influenced him in that direction. As he matured, Boisen cast a critical eye on his Calvinist rearing as well as on the tenants of theological liberalism as he experienced it in the early 20th century.

Consequentially, this middle road that Boisen took became the finite bordering on the infinite. It was the human boundary of the language of psychology and the language of traditional theology. He sought to relate the two voices, the vocabulary of psychology and the dynamic dialogue of theology, by trained observation and active listening to the narrative of "living human documents."

A **third** theological legacy was that crisis experiences, whether personal or social, "compel reorganization of person and group." This thesis was described in the book *Religion in Crisis and Custom* that he published in 1945. He believed that crisis experiences push back to what is "the universal and abiding, especially in social relatedness."[297] This was similar to Professor George Albert Coe's comment, "religious experience is rooted in the social nature of man and arises spontaneously under the pressure of crisis situations." Boisen said that in this context, "we frequently find contact with the ultimate reality to which we give the name God. This means a new awareness of the individual's continuity with society at its best."[298] This is also similar to what his professor at Union Seminary, Professor Coe contended; namely, that in whatever form religion takes, what happens is the recognition of the common or social will as *God in us*, and the recognition was like getting acquainted with a friend. For liberal theology, that friend was Jesus the Christ. One of the great contributions of liberal theology to Christianity was setting out the central place of Jesus the Christ as an actual historical Divine/human being through whom God acted for the salvation of humankind.

A **fourth** significant theological legacy is in Boisen's understanding of religious conversion. For Boisen, the acute schizophrenic experience marked the most dramatic transforming experience of his life. He upheld the belief that human salvation was rooted in the claim that what God intends to accomplish through the life, ministry, death, and in particular, the resurrection of Jesus is a lasting display of the depth of Divine Love. He accepted conversion as a reconstructive and creative religious experience of God active in love.

This led him to a particular interpretation of the atonement. For Boisen, the atonement was not a rescue mission on the part of Jesus. Nor was it the classical Ransom Theory of man and woman enslaved in bondage to sin. Boisen rejected the thought that the Good News was vicarious sacrifice as expiation of guilt, the strongly held Satisfaction and Substitution theories of the atonement that Jesus was a sacrificial victim. On the contrary, Jesus was "God active in love." To exist in God's love is to be with and for another.

In an article titled, "Cooperative Inquiry in Religion," printed in *Religious Education*, October 1945, he concluded his remarks with these words: "I believe that love is the paramount human need and that there is a law within which forbids us to be satisfied with any fellowship save that of the best religious experience, that is fellowship raised to its highest level."

A **fifth** legacy is for the religious person, the higher loyalty is represented by the idea of God. For Boisen this idea stands for something that is operative in the lives of all human beings, whether they recognize it or not.[299] The "idea of God" was both about community and about the highest values of human relationships. He deeply believed in the presence of God in his life and in the lives of those whom he loved. He transformed this divine/human story into a primary educational document. His first book published in 1936, *The Exploration of the Inner World,* is a tangible expression of that gift.[300] Boisen believed that to be isolated or estranged from God, and others, was to be condemned to a "death in the midst of life"[301] To be in the good company of a group whose *faith was active in love* became for Boisen the meaning of salvation.

Progressive Empiricist

What label might one give to Boisen as a theologian? Is he "mainline," "old-line," "liberal," "traditional," "conservative," "progressive," "evangelical"? What is a title for him as a theologian?

I have settled on the term **progressive empiricist** to describe him as a theologian.

Progressive: Christianity has always been progressive. The great theologians of the early church and the leaders of the high Middle Ages understood themselves to be progressive. Martin Luther thought of himself as recovering from the past what had been obscure. John Calvin presented a revolutionary new and progressive theology in the *Institutes of the Christian Religion.*

The years, just before the turn of the19th century and World War I, are known as the progressive years, or Progressive Era, in the United States. Boisen was a man of that time. He emphasized individual needs and the capacities, strengths and weakness, of each student and patient. The attitude one had toward another, how one another was treated, what one made of herself, was primary in human relationships. Boisen desired to be constantly in discourse with the common human experiences of life. Indeed, one of his progressive empirical methods was to create models, metaphors, symbols, and signs of the dominion of God.

Empiricist: He believed clergy should include in their preparation the "study of living human documents." His basic concern was that the use of theological language be in touch with concrete data of human experience. In theological education he advocated for the study of concrete religious experience accompanied by a deep concern for the welfare of troubled individuals.

What Boisen really wanted was to return to something like Dr. Friedrich Schleiermacher's empirical theology of religion as *experience*. Schleirmacher replaced revelation with religious feeling. Dr. Friedrich Schleiermacher (1768, 1834) was the father of empirical theology. His appeal was to religious *experience* derived from observation or experimental research. What Boisen wanted was to return to something like Freiderich Schliermacher's theology of religion as experience, "clearing up the channels of understanding within individuals and between individuals." To paraphrase Dr. Glenn Asquith, Jr., Boisen uses *experience* as a way of testing the *essence* of beliefs about God, sin, and salvation.[302] The revelation of Boisen's theological experience was the discovery of the potential for power within powerlessness, the very meaning of the crucifixion-resurrection event in Christian theology.

In a *Boisen-Dicks Lecture* for the Association of Professional Chaplains in May of 2006, Dr. John Patton, PhD, Director of Pastoral Counseling for the Georgia Association for Pastoral Care in Atlanta, Georgia spoke: "Wisdom for Anton Boisen did not grow out of the chaplain's association with health care or the psychological knowledge of the physician or psychoanalyst. It came instead from the power of relationship to reach out and affirm the humanness of the separated ones—those trapped in loneliness, confusion and powerlessness."[303]

Three Themes Present in Boisen's Theology
1. He saw the Bible and human experience metaphorically, meaning that it was more than literal, more than factual.

2. He sought the inner meaning of the Bible as it corresponded to the inner meaning of human experience.
3. He trusted human transformation through religious conversion as the beginning of a relationship with God and communal contextual existence with others - The Fellowship of the Best - that altered life in the here and now.

Narrative Theology

To bring Anton Boisen directly to the present, he was a pioneer in what we call today Narrative Theology. In contemporary theological circles, there is heightened interest in looking at human life structured by narrative. How we interpret, think, and make decisions is based on a narrative understanding of life. We make sense of life through the stories we tell. The Reverend Dr. Stanley Hauerwas, Professor of Theological Ethics at Duke Divinity School, is a strong proponent of narrative theology. He wrote in the book, *The Peaceable Kingdom*, "Christian convictions take the form of a story, or perhaps better a set of stories, that constitute a tradition, which in turn creates and forms a community. The calling of our attention to a narrative that tells of God's dealing with creation is a complex story with many subplots and digressions. My contention is that the narrative mode is neither incidental nor accidental to Christian belief. There is no more fundamental way to talk of God than in story."[304]

Boisen's legacy is that he believed that the story of a person can have meaning by the discipline of theological hermeneutics. Narrative theology can provide a language by which we connect the inner world of the other person to the outer world of experience and life events. For Boisen, the insight into the "living human document," the depth experiences in the struggles of an individual's mental and religious life, corresponded to analysis of the historic texts, such as the Gospels, at the foundation of the Christian faith. By listening to the story of human lives theology developed ideas with confidence.

Human experience was tested against the validity of theological formulations. In the light of the focus on narrative theology, and his new and crisp theological methodology, Boisen's contribution takes on important theological significance for our time.

In Sum

For Boisen, theological method was a new empirical approach to the age-old theological questions. Of utmost importance was the theologizing that comes as a result of soul care to individuals in need. Without these data of human experience there would be no theology for Boisen. [305]

By his method he gave theology a fresh expression, placing it in a live and vibrant context of human experience that led theology back from the total head level to the stimulating heart level. His was a theological viewpoint that not only reflected the empirical theology of the liberals of his day, but also echoed the grounding he had in the traditional theology of the Reformed Presbyterians of his childhood.[306]

16

MEMORY OF ANTON THEOPHILUS BOISEN

"The American Pioneer in Religion and Mental Health"

Photo through courtesy of Hammond Library Boisen
Collection CTS
**Theological Students and Supervisors at Elgin State
Hospital in 1937**

ANTON THEOPHILUS BOISEN:

In a speech at a meeting of the Council for Clinical Training and Theology Conference at Worcester State Hospital, Boisen said: "For the launching of this undertaking, I can myself claim no credit. It came about through no special merit or planning of my own. Ten years ago, I could have looked forward to see myself talking at this place on this subject, and I should have considered it as the wildest of wild dreams. As all of us here know, I was just picked up bodily and dumped down into this little-known country that we are now trying to explore. What has happened since has just worked it out step by step, and if we are now a going concern the credit must go very largely to the splendid group of helpers who have come to the rescue."[307] What happened was that clinical pastoral education became "unambiguously committed to theological education."[308]

Anton Boisen made three distinct and important contributions to the clinical pastoral education movement in his time.

> *First,* he believed that scientific research and empirical exploration of the life stories of individuals in crisis would bring about new ways for students to be challenged to think theologically about their encounters with individuals in need.
>
> *Second,* he believed that clinical pastoral education should strive to be a part of theological education, and not general training for counseling technique or psychological therapy, interpersonal skill learning, and the ability to relate was secondary to carrying out of such a goal.
>
> *Third,* he contributed the idea that listening to the narrative of the lives of people could reinforce the fundamental structures of traditional theology providing convincing implications for the care of souls

MEMORY OF ANTON THEOPHILUS BOISEN

Out of his own episodes of catatonic schizophrenia, Boisen believed that there was a religious dimension to mental illness; and he plunged himself into a life-long study of the inner world, challenging theological students and clergy to be engaged in a practical, here-and-now approach to the lives of patients and parishioners. This became a journey of clarifying theology on the basis of experience with individuals in crisis. Exploring the many paths he traveled, he discovered his own path; and, in time, he affirmed his own authority, wisdom, and methodology. Boisen believed that there is an offer given by God for greater spiritual integration in moments of crisis.[309]

He had the courage to champion a practical method of doing theological education not with ready-made theological formulations: "I have sought to begin not with the ready-made formulations contained in books but with the living human documents and with actual social conditions in all their complexity."[310] He challenged formal theological education in ways not initially shared by others. His theology was grounded in an empirical inquiry that does not hide strangeness but attends to it all in all its particularity. In the depths, he was soundly orthodox without being conservative. He was progressively liberal while engaging in difficult listening to enemies with costly love for them. The student learned a method of doing theology that could be understood and practiced in concrete human relationships. He taught that theology is conversation, conversation between text and event, between reading of the Bible and daily encounter with living human beings

Dr. Cushman McGiffert Jr. said that the impact of Anton Boisen on theological education centered in four basic aspects:

1. Boisen made the seminary student "shock-proof" in preparation for the parish.

2. Boisen helped students begin to understand themselves better.

3. Boisen had a practice of good soul-care.

4. Boisen cooperated with other professionals to provide a contextual environment for learning.[311]

On June 6, 1957, Boisen was honored by Chicago Theological Seminary with the honorary degree of Doctor of Letters, *honoris causa*. Dr. McGiffert, President of the seminary at that time, and long-time friend of Boisen, had these words to speak about Anton Theophilus Boisen:

> Anton T. Boisen, for whom the artificial boundary lines between fields of knowledge are not obstructive fences, but something to cross over; in whose mind the sciences of theology, psychology, and sociology keep company together; one-time explorer of frightening abysses of the human spirit; who has returned with new understanding and healing; to whose pioneering generations of students acknowledge indebtedness; former colleague, present friend, and mentor of many here assembled and across the miles: On recommendation of the Administrative Council and by the authority of the Board of Directors of the Chicago Theological Seminary, I confer upon you the degree of Doctor of Letters, *honoris causa*.[312]

Boisen's ideas about mental illness and the importance of the religious dimension in the treatment of mental illnesses have relevance for the twenty first century. A renewal of Boisen's perspective would contribute to the medical world an assessment of the whole person rather than just the organic manifestation of illness.

MEMORY OF ANTON THEOPHILUS BOISEN

Reverend Dr. Frederic M. Norstad, former Professor of Practical Theology at Luther Seminary in St. Paul, Minnesota, Vice President at Lutheran General Hospital and Program Director of the Lutheran Institute of Human Ecology in Park Ridge, Illinois during my chaplaincy at LGH in the 1970s wrote: "From both theology and modern science we derive our conviction that man is a complex inter-relationship of physical, mental, emotional, social and spiritual factors. These factors cannot be understood except in terms of their inseparable inter-action. Man influences, and is influenced by these forces. The practice of human ecology addresses the spiritual, social, mental, physical, and emotional aspect of human beings."[313]A renewal of Boisen's perspective would challenge the theological student to probe deeper into the relationship of theology to the spiritual, social, physical, emotional, and mental forces of "living human documents."

Reverend Clarence Bruninga, a former student of Boisen, stated that just prior to Boisen's death, he had a mental breakdown. It was in 1962. He had been sick and very depressed. That seemed to send him into the nether world for a brief period of time.[314] He was not hospitalized, but he had lived on the borderline of being and non-being since that time. Psychotic content came to the forefront with his fear of nuclear war, and many death thoughts, and his never resolved love affair with Alice.[315]

At Elgin State Hospital, Boisen lived in a room just off the kitchen down a long corridor. His room was not very clean. He used a wheel chair. There was a total lack of privacy. Fr. Henri Nouwen paid a visit; and he wrote that "there is no door, only a screen and the dishwashing noise in the kitchen intruded upon our conversation." Anton himself was friendly and he kept expressing thanks to the hospital for letting him live in this room after his retirement. His language was slow and often difficult to understand. He expressed his own irritation with not being able to put his thoughts in better words."[316]

Nouwen asked him, "Who is God?" His reply was: "God is the internalization of the highest values of our social relationship and Jesus Christ is the man in whom the Apostles found these highest values represented." He spoke of his own theology as liberal. Nouwen stated that he showed a preoccupation with the end of the world and his own personal death.

Anton Boisen died at Elgin State Hospital on October 2, 1965. He was almost eighty-nine years old. He died, as he had lived most of his life, alone.

Committal Service

There was a committal service at the Hilltop Cemetery at the Elgin State Hospital at which time part of his ashes were strewn over the grounds of the cemetery. Reverend Donald Beatty, a long time colleague at Elgin State Hospital, paid tribute to the life of Anton Boisen. Beatty said: "It should be remembered, in assessing the value of Boisen's pioneer work, that in 1925 there were very few full-time chaplains in general and mental hospitals; and there were almost none where the incumbent had specific training for this specialized ministry. How different is the situation now only a scant forty years later. Our Association was in very large measure influenced by Boisen and those who had come into this field of ministry either directly or indirectly by virtue of his influence."

Describing Anton Boisen's funeral, Thomas Klink said, "The scene was not spectacular, today. The weather was modestly autumnal and the sky just ordinarily overcast. Except for the cluster of awkward mourners, forty or fifty people including Chaplain Charles Sullivan, Acting President of Chicago Theological Seminary, Dr. Victor

Obenhaus, a few patients, a handful of friends, a few hospital staff, and a little group of ex-students and CPE supervisors." Reverend Jim Gibbons attended the funeral and he said, "the occasion was quiet, quick, informal, but solemn." He recalled that "those present were invited to take a handful of his ashes and scatter them on the Potter's Field. Many years later we found what remained of those ashes in a file drawer in the Boisen room at Chicago Theological Seminary."[317]

"There were no tears. There was little conversation, but because he lived and suffered and imposed his always-distant urgency on others, some of the living seem less likely to be scattered as burned-out ashes 'back of the hospital,' over the fallow waste ground."[318]

At a subsequent worship service sponsored by the Institute of Pastoral Care and the Council for Council Training at a national meeting in Miami, Florida on October 25, 1965 tribute was paid to Anton T. Boisen, memorial flowers were contributed by the Council for Church and Ministry of the United Church of Christ and ministers and Deacons from Old South Church, Boston. *The Litany of Tribute* ended with these words:

Almighty and most merciful God may our appreciation of Anton Boisen's life, faith, and work be your voice speaking to us. And may it minister to a truer and greater effort on our part to walk humbly in your sight, being ever mindful that our lives are much richer because Anton lived among us, much wiser because he gave of his wisdom, and much more meaningful because he taught us of your presence in our lives. Amen

A Service of interment for the remaining ashes of Anton T. Boisen was held on April 23, 1974. Acting President, Dr. Victor Obenhaus presided. His ashes are at Chicago Theological Seminary,

ANTON THEOPHILUS BOISEN:

Clarence Sidney Funk Cloisters, Chicago, Illinois.

With fullness of dedication, Anton Boisen used his own suffering as a servant model for other sufferers. Although painfully shy and isolated, he deepened insight into the nature of the human predicament and the religious response through the study of living human documents. He believed that "the end of life is to solve problems and add to the general welfare." He indeed did that. Boisen's life, work, impact, and legacy helped lay the foundation for the clinical pastoral education movement. We are all better off for having his presence still with us after all these many years.

By:

Reverend Robert David Leas

Honorably Retired Presbyterian Church USA

Certified Supervisor ACPE, Emeritus

History Manager

Association for Clinical Pastoral Education, Inc

December 2008

(Endnotes)

1. There are several short essays on the life of Anton T. Boisenindicating that he came from an academic family on both sides. I intend to picture the family in Bloomington and demonstrate the impact of his father, mother, and grandfather on his personal and religious development.

2. Professor Glenn Asquith, Jr., correspondence with author, November 2007.

3. The Association for Clinical Pastoral Education, Inc., "ACPE History Corner," *ACPE: The Association for Clinical Pastoral Education, Inc.*, http://www.acpe.edu/cpehistory.htm (accessed September 13, 2008).

4. Dante Alighieri, *The Divine Comedy* (New York: The American Library, Penguin Books, 1954), 16.

"In the middle of the journey of my life,

I found myself in a dark wood,

For I had lost the right path,

Oh how hard it is to tell what a wild, rugged, and harsh wood it was!

The very thought of it pierced

My heart with fear,

Oh so terrible, that death is hardly worse."

5. Henri J. M. Nouwen, "Anton T. Boisen and Theology through Living Human Documents," *Pastoral Psychology* 19, no. 186 (1968): 50.

6. Anton Boisen, *Out of the Depths* (New York: Harper and Brothers, 1960), 202.

7. Edward J. Larson, *Summer for the Gods* (New York: Basic Books, 2007), 21-24.

8. Anton Boisen, *Problems in Religion and Life: A Manual for Pastors* (New York: Abingdon-Cokesbury Press, 1946), 6.

9. Charles Gerkin, *The Living Human Document* (Nashville: Abingdon Press, 1984), 19.

10. Douglas John Hall, *Thinking the Faith* (Minneapolis: Fortress Press, 1991), 75-78.

11. Benjamin Weininger, *Medical Record for Anton T. Boisen* (Baltimore: Sheppard and Pratt Hospital, 1935), box 195, no. 2858, Pitts Theological Library, Emory University, Atlanta, GA.

12. John Patton, *Pastoral Care in Context* (Louisville, KY: Westminster /John Knox Press, 1993), 148.

13. Boisen, *Out of the Depths*, 202.

14. Weininger, *Medical Record for Anton T. Boisen*.

15. George Coe, *The Psychology of Religion* (Chicago: University of Chicago Press, 1916), 262.

16. Boisen, *Out of the Depths*, 205.

17. Paul Pruyser, "Anton T. Boisen and the Psychology of Religion," *Journal of Pastoral Care* 21, no. 4 (December 1967): 214; Henri J. M. Nouwen, "Anton T. Boisen and Theology through Living Human Documents," *Pastoral Psychology* 19, no. 186 (September 1968): 50.

18. Dr. Glenn Asquith, Jr., "The Clinical Method of Theological Inquiry of Anton. T. Boisen," (PhD dissertation, University Microfilms, Ann Arbor, MI, 1976) 61-67. Also in Brian Grant,

Schizophrenia: A Source of Social Insight (Philadelphia: Westminster Press, 1975), 213.

19. Julian Silverman, "When Schizophrenia Helps," *Psychology Today* 4, no. 4 (September 1970): 63, quoted in Glenn Asquith, Jr., "The Clinical Method of Theological Inquiry of Anton. T. Boisen," (PhD dissertation, University Microfilms, Ann Arbor, MI, 1976) 61-67. Also in Brian Grant, *Schizophrenia: A Source of Social Insight* (Philadelphia: Westminster Press, 1975), 63.

20. Anton Boisen, remarks at the Silver Anniversary Conference of the Council for Clinical Training of Theological Students, October 1950, quoted in Anton Boisen, "The Period of Beginnings," *The Journal of Pastoral Care* 5, no. 1 (Spring 1951): 14.

21. James H. Madison, "Old Times and New Times in Bloomington," in *Bloomington Past and Present,* by Will Counts, James H. Madison, and Scott Sanders, 19-20 (Bloomington: Indiana University Press, 2002).

22. Madison., "Old Times and New Times in Bloomington," 20-21.

23. Boisen, *Out of the Depths*, 21-22.

24. Boisen, Silver Anniversary Conference Remarks, in "The Period of Beginnings," 16.

25. Anton Boisen comments on the religious environment of Bloomington and Monroe County in "Divided Protestantism in a Midwest Country, A Study in the Natural History of Organized Religion," *Journal of Religion* 20, no. 4 (October 1940). Also, he reviewed early Presbyterianism in Bloomington, Indiana in a lecture he gave at the 100th anniversary of the United Presbyterian Church in Bloomington in 1933, "One Hundredth Anniversary of the Presbyterian Church in Bloomington, 1833 to 1933," Boisen Collection, Chicago Theological Seminary Hammond Library, Chicago, Illinois.

26. Hermann Boisen, *Preparatory Book of German Prose* (New York: D. C. Heath, 1882), Preface page 3. The main text is in German. The full text of this book is available online at http://books.google.com/books?id=w1gBAAAAYAAJ&printsec=frontcover&dq=%22 Preparatory+Book+of+German+Prose%22&ei=DzDhSI3TKpW0yQS89_DJCw (accessed September 29, 2008).

27. Hermann Boisen, *Notes to the Preparatory Book of German Prose* (Martha's Vineyard, Massachusetts: Modern Languages, 1882).

28. Anton Boisen, *Out of the Depths*, 24-26.

29. Boisen, *Out of the Depths*, 39.

30. Theophilus Wylie, *Indiana University: A History from 1820 to 1860* (Indianapolis: William Buford Printer, 1880), 138-139.

31. Anton Boisen to Dr. Noble at Sheppard and Enoch Pratt Hospital, December 10, 1935, Boisen Collection, Chicago Theological Seminary Hammond Library, Chicago, Illinois.

32. Keith Clay, Professor of Biology and Director of the Research and Teaching Preserve at Indiana University, wrote, "The trailing arbutus is an unassuming plant that has been entangled with Indiana University history for more than 100 years. From botanical explorations by faculty and students in the 1800s to co-ed adventures at Arbutus Hill at the turn of the century and 21st-century conservation efforts at Indiana University's new Research and Teaching Preserve, the trailing arbutus is part of Indiana University's past, present, and future." Botanically, the plant is a member of the blueberry family that is confined in Indiana to the Dunes region and a few south-central counties, primarily Monroe and Morgan.

33. Hermann Boisen, "Obituary," *Journal of Education* (1884), Bloomington, Indiana, Herman B Wells Library, Indiana University, E460.

34. Anton Boisen, "A List of the Locations Where Arbutus May

be Found to Accompany the Map," annotations to

35. "Distribution of Trailing Arbutus in Monroe County, Indiana in 1905 sketched from memory by A.T. Boisen, 1960." The Herman B Wells Library Archives, Indiana University, Bloomington, Indiana.

Henri J. M. Nouwen, "The Arbutus Flower," Series III, 31 – 168, mimeographed copy, The Henri J.M. Nouwen Archives and Research Collection, John M. Kelly Library, University of St. Michael's College, Toronto, Canada.

36. Boisen, *Out of the Depths*, 51.

37. Boisen, *Out of the Depths*, 56-57.

38. Boisen, *Out of the Depths*, 64.

39. One cold and gray afternoon in February of 2008, my friend Gene Stern and I went out east of Bloomington to seek Arbutus Hill. The directions Boisen left with his map of the arbutus sittings were helpful; however, the surrounding area is now built over with housing developments.

40. Sheppard and Enoch Pratt Hospital, *Medical Record for Anton T. Boisen*, Boisen Collection, Hammond Library, Chicago Theological Seminary, Chicago, Illinois.

41. L.C. Rudolph, *Hoosier Zion: The Presbyterians in Early Indiana* (New Haven: Yale University Press, 1963), 192.

42. Robert Hastings Nichols, *Presbyterianism in New York State* (Philadelphia: Westminster Press, 1953), 116-123.

43. The Old School Presbyterians were conservative. They generally opposed cooperation with the independent missionary groups such as the American Home Missionary Society and other ecumenical efforts for a Plan of Union with the Congregational Church.

44. "One Hundredth Anniversary of the Presbyterian Church in Bloomington, 1833 to 1933," Boisen Collection, Hammond

Library, Chicago Theological Seminary, Chicago, Illinois. This is a finely printed leather bound volume of the activity at the 100th celebration that took place in 1933.

45. *About Theophilus Adam Wylie*, Wylie House Museum, The Trustees of Indiana University, 1997-2003

46. Andrew Wylie, letter to Theophilus Wylie, 29 March 1837.

47. James Albert Woodburn, *History of Indiana University 1820-1902* (Bloomington, Indiana: Indiana University Press, 1940). Research Collections, UGL and University Archives: LD2518.WD.

48. Theophilus Wylie, *Indiana University: History from 1820 to 1860* (Indianapolis: W.B. Buford Printers, 1890).

49. Anton Boisen to Philip Guiles, Christmas Card, n.d., Austin Philip Guiles Papers, Correspondence, b MS 688, Box 5, Andover-Harvard Theological Library, Harvard Divinity School, Cambridge, Massachusetts.

50. James Albert Woodburn, "United Presbyterian Beginnings," *Indiana Magazine of History* 30, no. 1 (March 1954). The Reformed Presbyterian Church (Covenanter) is the remnant of those that hold to the whole of the Reformed church as existed in Scotland between the years 1638 and 1649. See also the *National Covenant* (1638) and *Solemn League and Covenant* (1643).

51. H. L. Smith, "The Underground Railroad in Monroe County" (Monroe, MI: Monroe County Historical Society, n.d.). In the years immediately preceding the Civil War, members of this Covenanter church were active supporters of the Underground Railroad in Indiana, assisting runaway slaves to escape to freedom and frequently hiding them in their own home.

52. As of 2008, there are still three different Presbyterian Churches in Bloomington.

53. Anton Boisen, "Divided Protestantism in a Midwest County: A Study in the Natural History of Organized Religion," *Journal of*

Religion 20, no. 4 (October 1940), quoted in Glenn Asquith, Jr., "Anton Boisen and 'The Study of Living Human Documents,'" *Journal of Presbyterian History* 60, no. 3 (1982): 266-247.

54. W.A. Hoffecker, "Old School Theology," *Religious Information Source*, http://mb-soft.com/believe/txc/oldschoo.htm (accessed February 2007).

55. Mrs. Floyd Aspen and Joseph Kingsbury, *Between Then and Now: 1819-1969, 150 Years of Presbyterians in Perspective* (Bloomington, Indiana: First Presbyterian Church, 1969), 12-17.

56. Jo Burgess, Director of the Wylie House Museum in Bloomington, Indiana, personal communication with author, March 3, 2004.

57. Theophilus A. Wylie, *The Diaries of Theophilus A. Wylie* (Bloomington, Indiana: Indiana University Office of Publications, n.d.).

58. Anton Boisen, "Fidelity and Vision" (paper presented on the 100th anniversary of the First Presbyterian Church in Bloomington, Indiana, September 25, 1933.

59. Dedication brochure for First Presbyterian Church's Second Century Recognition at Sixth and Lincoln Streets (1901-2001). The brochure was obtained on April 12, 2004. Walnut Street Presbyterian Church burned down in 1899, with many of the records and much of the interior destroyed. The new church was built on at Sixth and Lincoln near downtown Bloomington; the minister at that time was The Reverend M. G. Alison. An Indiana University faculty member and an administrator, The Reverend Baynard Hall (1825-1829) and The Reverend Andrew Wylie (1829-1834), served as pastors of this church in the early nineteenth century.

60. *Manual of the Walnut Street Presbyterian Church* (Bloomington, Indiana: 1893), First Presbyterian Church archives, Bloomington, Indiana.

61. Invitation to the home of The Reverend Mr. and Mrs. George Luccock, September 4, 1893, Bloomington, Indiana, Archives of Indiana University.

62. Anton Boisen's theology became a mixture of the Reformed theology and tradition of his grandfather and the Liberal theology of the early twentieth century, as experienced in worship with his mother and as taught at Union Seminary by Coe and Brown.

63. Elizabeth Louisa Wylie to Jane Wylie, Indiana University Archives, Herman B Wells Library, Bloomington, Indiana.

64. Elizabeth Louisa Wylie to Jane Wylie, Indiana University Archives, Herman B Wells Library, Bloomington, Indiana.

65. Elizabeth Louisa Wylie to Jane Harris, Indiana University Archives, Herman B Wells Library, Bloomington, Indiana.

66. Arbutus Yearbook, 1900 (Bloomington: Indiana University), Indiana University Archives. The yearbook lists Marie as a graduate in English.

67. *Arbutus Yearbook,* 1897 (Bloomington, Indiana: Indiana University), Indiana University Archives. The yearbook lists Anton Boisen as graduating in the German Department, along with five other students.

68. Boisen, *Out of the Depths,* 47.

69. William James, *The Varieties of Religious Experience* (New York: The Modern Library, 1994), 36 and 40.

70. James, *The Varieties of Religious Experience,* 157.

71. Freud, Sigmund, *Introductory Lectures on Psychology, Standard Edition* (New York, NY: W.W. Norton, 1965), 444-445.

72. "Anton T. Boisen, Yale Forest School, Graduating Class of 1905," *Biographical Record of the Graduates and Former Students of the Yale Forest School* (New Haven: Yale Forest School, 1913), 95, Forest History Society, Inc.,701 William Vickers Avenue, Durham, NC 27701, Cheryl Oakes, Archivist.

ENDNOTES

73. *United States Department of Agriculture, Forest Service, Field Program Reports 1905 to 1908*, Gifford Pinchot, Chief Forester, Durham, North Carolina: Forest History Society, Inc.

74. Anton Boisen and J. A. Newlin, "Commercial Hickories," (Washington D. C: Department of Agriculture Bulletin 80, Henry Graves, Forester, 1910), deposited in Boisen Collection, Hammond Library, Chicago Theological Seminary, Chicago, Illinois, also found online, http://www.archive.org/stream/commercialhickor00boisrich/commercialhickor00boisrich_djvu.txt

75. Henri Nouwen, "Anton T. Boisen and Theology through Living Human Documents," *Pastoral Psychology*, September 1968, quoted in Glenn Asquith, Jr., ed., *Vision from a Little Known Country* (Atlanta, Georgia: Journal of Pastoral Care Publications, 1992).

76. Anton Boisen to Francis McPeek, September 28, 1940, private collection.

77. "Alumni Notes," *Yale Forest School News* 35 (July 3, 1947), Graves Forestry and Environmental Studies Library, Yale University, New Haven, Connecticut.

78. Anton Boisen and Frederick Eastman, "A Rural Survey in Missouri" (New York, NY: Department of Church and Country Life of the Board of Home Missions of the Presbyterian Church in the U.S.A., 1911), Widener Library, Harvard University, Cambridge, Massachusetts, also on line, http://www.archive.org/details/ruralsurveyinmis00pres

79. George Coe, *The Psychology of Religion* (Chicago: University of Chicago Press, 1916).

80. Anton Boisen, "Clinical Pastoral Training in Retrospect and Prospect" (lecture, faculty luncheon of Union Seminary, New York, NY, October 30, 1957), mimeographed copy in the Boisen

Collection, Hammond Library, Chicago Theological Seminary, Chicago, Illinois.

81. Robert C. Powell, *Anton Boisen*, supplement to the *American Mental Heath Chaplains Forum* 29, no. 1(October 1976): 7.

82. Adolph Mayer was a strong believer in the importance of empiricism, and advocated repeatedly for a scientific approach to understanding mental illness. Mayer became so influential in the USA that he was known as "the dean of American psychiatry," and his work has had a wide influence on psychiatric theory and practice. In Mayer's view, the diagnosis and treatment of a mental disorder must include a thorough understanding of the patient as a whole person (CNET Networks, Inc. All Rights Reserved, 2007).

83. Henri J. M. Nouwen, "Boisen and Coe," Archives and Research Collection of Essays, University of St. Michael's College, Toronto, Ontario.

84. Boisen was a classmate of Socialist Norman Thomas, who attended Union Theological Seminary and there adopted his socialist convictions. Thomas was ordained as a Presbyterian minister in 1911. He ministered to an Italian Protestant Church in New York's East Harlem. Union Theological Seminary was then a center of the Social Gospel movement and liberal politics.

85. The Socialist Party of the United States of America was formally organized at a unity convention in Indianapolis in 1901. The two merging groups were the Social Democratic Party of Eugene Victor Debs, a Terre Haute, Indiana-born activist, and the pre-existing Socialist Labor Party. The SDP had been organized in 1898 by veterans of the Pullman strike of the American Railway Union, led by Eugene Debs. After World War I, weakened by the loss of the Bolsheviks, the Socialist Party did not run a Presidential candidate in 1924; however, in 1926, the Socialist Party revived as an independent electoral entity under the leadership of Norman

ENDNOTES

Thomas, an opponent of World War I, and a founder of the American Civil Liberties Union. After the death of Eugene Debs in 1926 Norman Thomas was the presidential candidate for the Socialist Party in 1928, 1932 and 1936.

86. Union Seminary in New York City had broken with the Presbyterian Church on the issue of Biblical inerrancy close to the time Anton was there. This crisis centered on William A. Brown's unwillingness to ascribe to Biblical literalism. (Reverend Joan Hemenway to the author, March 2005).

87. Boisen, *Out of the Depths*, 4.

88. Anton Boisen, "Clinical Pastoral Training in Retrospect and Prospect," Boisen Collection, Hammond Library, Chicago Theological Seminary, Chicago, Illinois. In this document he refers to his ordination by the Brookline Presbytery. Today the presbytery is the Presbytery of Boston, Synod of the Northeast, with offices at Newton Center, Massachusetts.

89. In correspondence with the Librarian at the Congregational Library in Boston, Mr. Harold Worthley, he indicates that Boisen transferred his ministerial standing from the Presbyterian to the Congregational denomination in 1912.

90. Boisen and Eastman, "A Rural Survey in Missouri." (New York: Redfield Brothers, Inc. 1911), Cambridge, Widener Library, Harvard University, 27, also on line, http://www.archive.org/details/ruralsurveyinmis00pres

91. The Reverend Warren Wilson was a graduate of Oberlin College and Union Seminary. He had a PhD degree in Sociology from Columbia University in New York City. He was Secretary of the Department of Church and Country Life in the Presbyterian Church. His largest survey was in Ohio, where he joined with Washington Gladden, the Prophet of the Social Gospel, to initiate

inter-denominational cooperation before the Federal Council of Churches of Christ in America.

92. Warren Wilson, "The Church and Rural Community," *American Journal of Sociology* (March 1911): 668-93.

93. James H. Madison, "Reformers and the Rural Church," *Journal of American History* 73, no. 3 (December 1986): 645.

94. Madison, "Reformers," 643.

95. Anton T. Boisen and Fred Eastman, "A Rural Survey in Missouri," 27.

96. Boisen and Eastman, "A Rural Survey in Missouri."20

97. Boisen and Eastman, "A Rural Survey in Missouri," 34-35

9898. Anton T. Boisen, "A Rural Survey in Tennessee" (New York: Redfield Brothers, Inc. 1912), Cambridge, Widener Library, Harvard University, also on line, www.archive.org/details/ ruralsurveyinmis00pres

99. Boisen, "A Rural Survey in Tennessee," 40-42.

99100 Boisen, "A Rural Survey in Tennessee." 45.

100

101101. Boisen, "A Rural Survey in Missouri," 26.

102. Boisen, "A Rural Survey in Missouri" 38.

103. Anton Boisen, "Factors Which Have to do with the Decline of the Country Church," *The American Journal of Sociology* 22, no. 2 (September 2, 1916): 191-192.

104. Anton Boisen, *In Defense of Mr. Bryan: A Personal Confession by a Disciple of Dr. Fosdick*, mimeographed copy from the Boisen Collection, file cabinet two, bottom drawer, Hammond Library, Chicago Theological Seminary, Chicago, Illinois.

105. Boisen, *Out of the Depths*, 77.

106. Boisen, *Out of the Depths*, 68-69.

107. Boisen, *Out of the Depths*, 71.

108. Boisen, *Out of the Depths*, 71.

ENDNOTES

109. Boisen, *Out of the Depths*, 73.

110. Boisen, *Out of the Depths*, 72-73.

111. John Piper, *Robert E. Speer, Prophet of the American Church* (Louisville: Geneva Press, 2000), 305-310, 312, 314.

112. James H. Madison, "Reformers and the Rural Church," *Journal of American History* 73, no. 3(December

1986): 664-665.

113. Henri J. M. Nouwen, "Anton Boisen and the Study of Theology," *Theology* 19, no. 186 (September 1968): 3.

114. Madison, "Reformers and the Rural Church," 667.

115. Edmund de S. Brunner, *As Now Remembered: The Interesting Life of an Average Man* (Bethlehem, Pennsylvania: Archives of the Moravian Brethren, Private Printing, 1968), 23.

116. Anton Boisen to Fred Kuether, Executive Director of the Council for Clinical Training, regarding entries in the Council for Clinical Training of Theological Students Catalogue for 1948, September 7, 1948, Box 195, no. 2847, Archives Collection for ACPE, Pitts Theological Library, Emory University, Decatur, Georgia.

117. Boisen, *Out of the Depths*, 56.

118. I hesitate to call it a "relationship," for there was no reciprocal love or affection on the part of Alice.

119. Henri J. M Nouwen, "Anton Boisen's Relationship to Alice Batchelder," Series III A. 7 Notes and Manuscripts regarding Boisen by Henri Nouwen (ca.1966-1975) 31-167, John M. Kelly Library, Archives and Research Collection, University of St. Michael's College, Toronto, Canada.

120. Boisen, *Out of the Depths*, 76.

121. Italics are my own.

122. Anton Boisen to Alice Batchelder, Saturday morning, July 24, 1920, Boisen Collection, Wooden cabinet of loose material,

Chicago Theological Seminary Hammond Library, Chicago, Illinois.

123. Alice Batchelder to Anton Boisen (n.d.), Boisen Collection, Hammond Library, Chicago Theological Seminary, Chicago, Illinois.

124. Boisen, *Out of the Depths*, 163-165.

125. Boisen, *Out of the Depths*, 49.

126. Glenn Asquith, Jr., *The Clinical Method of Theological Inquiry of Anton T. Boisen*, (PhD diss., Southern Baptist Seminary, 1976) Ann Arbor, Michigan: University Microfilms, 42-43.

127. Boisen, *Out of the Depths*, 176.

128. It would be difficult to confirm that Alice agreed to the document of disclosure.

129. Paraphrase from Dr. Robert C. Powell in a personal email on November 1, 2006. (Dr. Eugen Kahn MD was Sterling Professor of Psychiatry at Yale Medical School from 1930 to 1946. He received a medical degree from Munich in 1911.)

130. Anton Boisen to Catherine Wilson, June 15, 1936, mimeographed copy from Boisen Collection, Hammond Library, Chicago Theological Seminary, Chicago, Illinois.

131. Boisen to Wilson, June 15, 1936, p. 209.

132. Boisen to Wilson, June 15, 1936, p. 210.

133. Henri J. M. Nouwen wrote his doctoral dissertation on Anton Boisen at the Nijmegen University in the Netherlands. He was told it was not acceptable because it was not based on statistics and clinical models. Henri was angry and balked at this attempt to "straitjacket" him. He dropped the thesis and left Nijmegen with a *doctorandus* degree—a professional degree and not an academic research degree.

134. Henri J. M. Nouwen, "Anton Boisen's Relationship to Alice Batchelder," John M. Kelly Library, Archives and Research Collection, University of St. Michael's College, Toronto, Canada,

Series III, A. 7 Notes and Manuscripts by Nouwen re: Anton Boisen, (no date), 31-16.

135. Boisen, *Out of the Depths*, 139.

136. Boisen, *Out of the Depths*, 210.

137. John Lennart Cedarleaf, "Anton Boisen—A Memoir," *Cura Animarum* (Decatur, Georgia: Journal of Pastoral Care Publications, Inc., 1992), 61.

138. Anton Boisen, *Exploration of the Inner World* (New York: Willett Clark and Company, 1936), 115-116. Also *Clinical Pastoral Training in Retrospect and Prospect* (remarks, faculty luncheon at Union Seminary, October 30, 1957), mimeographed copy from Hammond Library, *Boisen Collection*, CTS.

139. Don Marshall, MD, read the draft of the manuscript for this biography. Today, his diagnosis of Boisen most likely would be of a "schizo-affective disorder." Boisen manifested symptoms for both schizophrenia and mood disorder (depression or manic behavior—bipolar).

140. Glenn Asquith, "Anton T. Boisen and the Study of Living Human Documents," *The Journal of Presbyterian History* 60, no. 3 (1982): 254.

141. Boisen, *Out of the Depths*, 82ff.

142. Boisen, *Out of the Depths*, 80.

143. Her departure from the Council was due in part to her Freudian and Reichian ideas. Hendrika Vande Kemp, "Helen Flanders Dunbar, 1902-1959," *The Feminist Psychologist: Newsletter of the Society for the Psychology of Women* 28, no. 1, Winter 2001: 2.

144. Boisen, *Out of the Depths*, 91.

145. Anton Boisen, "Clinical Pastoral Training in Retrospect and Prospect" (remarks, faculty luncheon at Union Theological Seminary, October 30, 1957), Boisen Collection, Hammond Library,

Chicago Theological Seminary, Chicago, Illinois.

146. Boisen, "Clinical Pastoral Training in Retrospect and Prospect."

147. Boisen, *The Exploration of the Inner World*, 1.

148. Edward Larson, *Summer for the Gods: The Scopes Trial and America's Continuing Debate over Science and Religion* (New York: Basic Books, 2006), 21-22.

149. Anton Boisen, "Theme of Our Objectives" (lecture before the Council for Clinical Training of Theological Students Conference, Worcester State Hospital, August 23, 1930), Archives for ACPE, Pitts Theological Library, Candler School of Theology at Emory University, Decatur, Georgia.

150. Henri J. M. Nouwen, "Boisen and Freud," mimeographed document, n.d., The Henri J. M. Nouwen Archives and Research Collection, John M. Kelly Library, University of St. Michael's College, Toronto, Canada.

151. Boisen, *Out of the Depths*, 103.

152. Boisen, *The Exploration of the Inner World*, 299.

153. Boisen, *The Exploration of the Inner World*, 59.

154. Hillman, James, *On Paranoia* (Putnam, CT: Eranos Foundation, Spring Publications, Inc., 1985), 10.

155. Lucy Bergman, "Anton Boisen Revisited," *Journal of Religion and Health* 18, no. 3 (1979): 213-229.

156. Boisen, *The Exploration of the Inner World*, 104-107.

157. Anton Boisen, *Studies of a Little Known Country*, file cabinet 5, back of drawer 1, Boisen Collection, Hammond Library, Chicago Theological Seminary, Chicago, Illinois.

158. Boisen, *Studies of a Little Known Country*, photo copy from Hammond Library, Chicago Theological Seminary, Chicago, Illinois(1922).

159. Wilhelm Maximilian Wundt instituted the first psychological

laboratory in 1878 at the University of Leipzig, Germany. He was also a powerful influence upon the founders of Pragmatism.

160. William Lowe Bryan served the longest presidency in Indiana University history, 1902 to 1937.

161. William Lowe Bryan to Anton Boisen, January 23, 1941, Wylie Collection, Indiana University Archives, Bloomington, Indiana.

162. Anton Boisen, *Religion in Crisis and Custom: A Sociological and Psychological Study* (New York: Harper and Brothers, 1945),12.

163. Richard Cabot, MD, "Adventures on the Borderland of Ethics: A Plea for a Clinical Year in the Course of Theological Study," in *Adventures on the Borderland of Ethics* (New York: Harper and Brothers, 1926).

164. Brian Grant, *Schizophrenia: A Source of Social Insight* (Philadelphia: Westminster Press, 1975), 95-96.

165. Anton Boisen, *Diary for 1924*, filing cabinet 5, top drawer, Boisen Collection, Hammond Library, Chicago Theological Seminary, Chicago, Illinois.

166. Boisen, *The Exploration of the Inner World*, 9.

167. Seward Hiltner, "The Debt of Clinical Pastoral Education to Anton T. Boisen," *The Journal of Pastoral Care* 20, no. 3 (September 1966): 130.

168. Rollin Fairbanks and Richard Cabot, *Pastoral Psychology*, March 1954: 30.

169. Anton Boisen to Fred Kuether, September 7, 1948, Pitts Theological Library, Emory University. "The earlier paper published January 1924 contains a direct reference to my work and was written in accordance with his plan to help me with the proposed research project at the Boston Psychopathic Hospital."

170. Dr. Helen Flanders Dunbar was Boisen's understudy for chaplains rather than a student in clinical training during the

summer of 1925. She stayed at Worcester for only one month.

171. Carroll Wise, "Worcester State Hospital,1932," Box 194, file 2245, Boisen Collection, Pitts Theological Library, Emory University, Atlanta, Georgia.

172. Homer Jernigan, "Clinical Pastoral Education in the Northeast 1925-2000," privately published booklet for the 75th Anniversary of the founding of CPE.

173. Anton Boisen, *Diary for 1927*, Boisen Collection, Hammond Library, Chicago Theological Seminary, Chicago, Illinois, 197.

174. Jernigan, *Clinical Pastoral Education in the Northeast*, 11-13.

175. Cabot, "A Plea for a Clinical Year in the Course of Theological Study," 4-22.

176. Larson, *Summer for the Gods*.

177. Anton Boisen, "In Defense of Mr. Bryan: A Personal Confession of a Disciple of Dr. Fosdick," (n.d.), 3, mimeographed copy, cabinet 1, bottom drawer, Boisen Collection, Hammond Library, Chicago Theological Seminary, Chicago, Illinois.

178. Asquith, "An Experiential Theology," in *Turning Points in Pastoral Care*, 22-23.

179. Anton Boisen, "In Defense of Mr. Bryan, a Personal Confession by a Disciple of Dr. Fosdick," (n.d.), 8-19, Boisen Collection, Hammond Library, Chicago Theological Seminary, Chicago, Illinois.

180. John Thomas, *Panel on Anton Boisen*, October 31, 1984, kept at ACPE Office, Decatur, Georgia, videotape.

181. Thomas, *Panel on Anton Boisen*.

182. John Lennart Cedarleaf, *The 50th Anniversary of the Pastoral Care and Education Movement*, Lexington, KY: University of Kentucky, Carnahan House, (1975), videotape.

183. Arthur Cushman McGiffert, Jr., "Memories of Anton Boisen," (remarks at Claremont School of Theology, Claremont,

California, July 24, 1986).

184. McGiffert, "Memories of Anton Boisen."

185. Hendrika Vande Kemp, *Harry Stack Sullivan (1892-1949): Hero, Ghost, and Muse* (Philadelphia, PA: Haworth Press. 2006), 31-35.

186. The list for the books noted were obtained one mid-November day, 2006, when I had the privilege of opening the boxes from his library in the attic of the Chicago Theological Seminary with Assistant Librarian Seon Hoen Lee.

187. Boisen, *Out of the Depths*, 184.

188. Carroll Wise, *Remarks at Lutheran General Hospital*, videotape (North Central Region History Committee, February 12, 1980), ACPE Office, Decatur, Georgia.

189. McCormick Theological Seminary to The Council for Clinical Training, May 9, 1942, regarding John Thomas's decision to train at Elgin State Hospital, private collection.

190. John Thomas, *Collaborative Efforts 1944-2005*, unpublished paper.

191. Anton Boisen, interview by McPeek, April 8, 1952, Pitts Theological Library, Candler School of Theology, Emory University, Atlanta, GA.

192. Paul Pruyser, *50th Anniversary of the Pastoral Care and Education Movement*, videotape (Carnahan House, University of Kentucky, 1975).

193. Anton Boisen, "Sermons," Boisen Collection, Hamilton Library, Chicago Theological Seminary, Chicago, Illinois.

194. Anton Boisen, "Presuppositions," pamphlet for *Hymns of Hope and Courage*, 4th ed. (Chicago, Illinois: Chicago Theological Seminary, 1959).

195. Anton Boisen, interview by McPeek.

196. John Lennart Cedarleaf, "Anton Boisen – A Memoir," *Cura Animaram* (Decatur, Georgia: Journal of Pastoral Care Publications, Inc., 1992), 60-61.

197. Anton Boisen, "The Service of Worship in a Mental Hospital: Its Therapeutic Significance," *Journal of Clinical Pastoral Work* 2, no. 1 (1948).

198. Boisen, "The Service of Worship in a Mental Hospital."

199. George Herbert Mead's view is communication through *significant symbols*. A significant symbol is a gesture (usually a vocal gesture) that calls out in the individual making the gesture the same (i.e., a functionally identical) response that is called out in others to whom the gesture is directed (*Mind, Self and Society*, 47). George Herbert Mead taught at the University of Chicago, the center of American Pragmatism, which had originated with Charles Sanders Peirce (1839-1914) and William James at Harvard. The "Chicago Pragmatists" were led by James Hayden Tufts, John Dewey, and George Herbert Mead. Dewey left Chicago for Columbia University in 1904, leaving Tufts and Mead as the major spokesmen for the Pragmatist movement at Chicago.

200. Boisen, *The Exploration of the Inner World*, 255-260.

201. Anton Boisen, foreword to *Hymns of Hope and Courage*, 4th ed. (Chicago, Illinois: Chicago Theological Seminary, Fourth Edition, 1956).

202. Powell, *Anton Boisen*, pp 26-27.

203. Dr. William A. Bryan was recognized for his leadership by the naming of the William A. Bryan Treatment Center. The commemorative plaque presented in 1957 reads: "The William A. Bryan Treatment Center, dedicated to the memory of the man who as Superintendent of this hospital from 1921 to 1940 constantly sought to improve methods of treatment."

204. Carroll Wise, *Presentation on Anton T. Boisen*, videotape

ENDNOTES

(Chicago: The Association for Clinical Pastoral Education Conference at Chicago Theological Seminary, 1984).

205. Carroll Wise, *Presentation at Lutheran General Hospital, Dr. Robert Powell presiding*, videotape (Lutheran General Hospital, February 12, 1980).

206. Robert C. Powell, MD, *Healing and Wholeness, Helen Flanders Dunbar and an Extra Medical Origin of the American Psychosomatic Movement, 1906-1936* (PhD dissertation, Duke University, 1974), 201, cited in Allison Stokes, *Ministry after Freud* (New York: The Pilgrim Press, 1985), 202 n.181.

207. Robert C. Powell, MD, *Healing and Wholeness: Helen Flanders Dunbar (1902-1959) and an Extra-medical Origin of the American Psychosomatic Movement, 1906-1936* (PhD dissertation, Duke University, 1974), 87-98.

208. Helen Flanders Dunbar, MD, "A Few Words Regarding the General Significance of the Newly Established Council for the Clinical Training of Theological Students," Pitts Theological Library, Candler School of Theology, Emory University, Atlanta Georgia.

209. Robert C. Powell, MD, "Emotionally, Soulfully, Spiritually Free to Think and Act" (The Helen Flanders Dunbar Memorial Lecture at Columbia Presbyterian Center, New York Presbyterian Hospital, NY, November 2, 1999) 5:98, published by *Theology and Health*, 2001.

210. Medieval Romance poetry and song includes *Erec and Enides, Cliges, Lancelot the Knight and the Cart, Yvain the Knight with the Lion,* and *Perceval and the Story of the Grail,* by French author Chrètien de Troyes around 1160 to 1190. A German retelling of the Grail legend is *Parzival* by the German author Wolfram Von Eschenbach around 1200. *Tristan and Iseult was* written by Thomas of Britain by 1170, and undoubtebly the most popular Romance story was

written around 1400, entitled *Sir Gawain and the Green Knight.* In the latter part of the 12th century, Robert de Boron from Burgundy composed a Grail romance trilogy, *Joseph d'Arimathie, Merlin,* and *Perceval.* About 1100 *The Song of Roland* appeared, probably the most famous piece of French Medieval literature, author unknown. Later, there is the English author, Sir Thomas Malory, who wrote *Morte d'Arthur* and *The Book of King Arthur and His Knights of the Round Table,* published in 1470.

211 . Henri J. M. Nouwen, "Boisen and Coe," (Nouwen Archives and Research Collection, University of Toronto), p. 14.

212. Anton Boisen, "The Genesis and Significance of Mystical Identification in Cases of Mental Disorder," *Psychiatry* 15, no. 3 (August 1952): 287, 294-295.

213. "Auto suggestion," *American Heritage Dictionary* (Boston, Massachusetts: Houghton Mifflin Company, 1985). A process by which an individual induces self-suggestion of an opinion, belief, or plan of action.

214. Anton Boisen, "The Genesis and Significance of Mystical Identification in Cases of Mental Disorder," *Psychiatry* 15, No. 3 (August 1952): 294, 295.

215. Boisen, *Exploration of the Inner World,* 147.

216. Boisen, *Out of the Depths,* 204-205.

217. Thornton, *Professional Education for Ministry,* 77.

218. Anton Boisen, *First Annual Report of the Chicago Council for Clinical Training of Theological Students,* mimeographed report, Boisen Collection, Hammond Library, Chicago Theological Seminary, Chicago, Illinois.

219. Simultaneous to this there was a "falling out" among the leaders of what became the Institute for Pastoral Care. Dr. Cabot no longer trusted Anton's judgment and his leadership, and a break occurred between the two. Cabot would have nothing to do with

those who believed that mental illness was due to inner psychiatric problems in living.

220. Edward Thornton, *Professional Education for Ministry* (Nashville: Abingdon Press, 1979), 62-64.

221. Homer L. Jernigan, *Clinical Pastoral Education in the Northeast 1925-2000* (privately published, 2000).

222. Anton Boisen was actually the first appointee to a seminary faculty as a clinical educator, but he was not a full-time faculty member at Chicago Theological Seminary.

223. Fritz Norstad, interview by Charles Hall, 1987, *Head and Heart*, Charles Hall (Decatur, Georgia: Journal of Pastoral Care Publications, Inc., 1992).

224. Thornton, Edward, *Professional Education for Ministry: A History of Clinical Pastoral Education* (New York: Abingdon Press, 1970), 90-91.

225. Anton Boisen to J. Willard Sperry, December 6, 1933, Series IV, Correspondence, b MS 688, Andover-Harvard Theological Library, Harvard Divinity School, Cambridge, Massachusetts.

226. Anton Boisen, "The Present Status of William James's Psychology of Religion," *Journal of Pastoral Care* 7, no. 3: 157.

227. Anton Boisen to Fred Kuether, late 1940s, private collection.

228. *Boisen Medical Record* (Baltimore, MD: Sheppard and Enoch Pratt Hospital), 3.

229. Anton Boisen to Dr. Noble, Sheppard and Enoch Pratt Hospital, December 10, 1935 Boisen Collection, Chicago, Illinois: Chicago Theological Seminary Library, separately bound document.

230. Boisen Medical Record (Baltimore, MD: Sheppard and Enoch Pratt Hospital), 3-4.

231. Rev.John Rae Thomas, "Biography of William Richardson Andrew, 1917-1969," in *Book of Remembrance for ACPE, Inc.* (1946).

232. The Rev. John Irving Smith continued the philosophy Boisen had propounded when he took over as the chaplain at Worcester in 1950. Smith was the first President of ACPE and the Interim Executive in 1967-68. He was elected Executive Director in 1968.

233. Fred Kuether became the first Director of Training at the Newly formed Blanton-Peale Institute at the Marble Collegiate Church in New York City in 1955.

234. Anton Boisen to Fred Kuether, September 21, 1954, Anton Boisen Collection, box 195, n.o. 2356, ACPE Archives, Pitts Theological Library, Emory University, Atlanta, Georgia.

235. Anton Boisen, "Conscientious Objectors," *Psychiatry* 7, no. 3 (August 1944).

236. William Lowe Bryan to Anton Boisen, n.d., file cabinet three, second drawer, Boisen Collection, Hammond Library, Chicago Theological Seminary, Chicago, Illinois.

237. Dr. Glenn Asquith Jr., *Building Bridges: A History of the Eastern Region of ACPE* (2000), 4. Asquith states that Boisen was rejected for certification as a supervisor by the Council in 1946.

238. Anton Boisen, *Pacific School of Religion Study,* file cabinet 3, second drawer, Boisen Collection, Hammond Library, Chicago Theological Seminary, Chicago, Illinois.

239. *Twenty-second Interdenominational Pastoral Conference* (Berkeley, California: The E. T. Earl Foundation and Pacific School of Religion, February 16-18, 1943), b MS 688 box 5, Austin Philip Guiles Papers, Andover-Harvard Library, Harvard Divinity School, Cambridge, Massachusetts.

240. Anton Boisen, *Social Action* (New York: Council for Social Action, the Congregational Christian Churches, March 15, 1939).

ENDNOTES

241. William F. Adix, *The Story of the Pacific Region* (Loma Linda, California: Loma Linda University Printing Services, 2000), 4.

242. A study of the Clinical Pastoral Education movement can be found in the following: Edward Thornton, *Professional Education for Ministry* (Nashville: Abingdon Press, 1970); E. Brooks Holifield, *A History of Pastoral Care in America* (Nashville: Abingdon Press, 1983); Allison Stokes, *Ministry after Freud* (New York: Pilgrim Press, 1985); Charles E. Hall, *Head and Heart* (Decatur, Georgia: Journal of Pastoral Care Publications, 1992); Joan Hemenway, *Inside the Circle: A Historical and Practical Inquiry Concerning Process Groups in Clinical Pastoral Education* (Decatur, Georgia: Journal of Pastoral Care Publications, 1996); Steven King, *Trust the Process: A History of Clinical Education as Theological Education* (New York: University Press of America, 2007).

243. Anton Boisen, "The Problem of Values in the Light of Psychopathology," *The American Journal of Sociology* 38, no. 3, (July 1932).

244. Anton Boisen, *Exploration of the Inner World*, 15-58.

245. Raphael Zon (1874-1956) helped build the U. S. Forest Service organization by promoting the importance of scientific investigation. Zon was instrumental in the creation of Forest Experiment Stations, and without doubt was the force behind scientific leadership in the U.S. Forest Service Agency in its formative years.

246. Henri J. M. Nouwen, "Boisen and the Case Method," *Chicago Theological Seminary Register* 67, no.1: 19.

247. A. D. Irvine, *Stanford Encyclopedia of Philosophy* (Stanford, California: Stanford University Press, 2006).

248. Allison Stokes, *Ministry after Freud* (New York: Pilgrim Press, 1985), 64 and 200.

249. William James, "What is Pragmatism? A Series of Eight Lectures Dedicated to the Memory of John Stuart Mill," Lecture 2 in *Pragmatism: A New Name for Some Old Ways of Thinking* (New York: The Library of America, 1904).

250. Cynthia Lanius: "A fractal is a pattern that reveals greater complication as it is enlarged. Thus, fractals graphically portray the notion of 'worlds within worlds.' Objects in nature often look fractal in structure. Most objects in nature aren't formed of squares or triangles, but of more complicated geometric figures. Many natural objects—ferns, coastlines, etc.—are shaped like fractals." Cynthia Lanius, "Cynthia Lanius' Lessons: A Fractals Lesson – Introduction," Department of Mathematics at Rice University, http://math.rice.edu/~lanius/frac (accessed October 1, 2008).

251. Charles Pierce, "How to Make Our Ideas Clear," *Popular Science Monthly,* January 1878, quoted in *"What Is Pragmatism? A Series of Eight Lectures Dedicated to the Memory of John Stuart Mill,"* in *A New Name for Some Old Ways of Thinking* (New York: The Library of America, 1904).

252. *The American Heritage Dictionary* (Boston: Houghton Mifflin Co., 1976), 122.

253. Anton Boisen, "An Experiment in Theological Education," in *Statement of the Aims and Accomplishments of the Council for Clinical Training in the Chicago Area.*(1935), box 194, folder 2846, Boisen Collection, Pitts Theological Library, Candler School of Theology, Emory University, Atlanta, Georgia.

254. "Toward the end of the 19th century, pragmatism became the most vital school of thought within American philosophy. It continued the empiricist tradition of grounding knowledge on experience and stressing the inductive procedures of experimental science. The pragmatists believed in the progress of human knowledge and that ideas are tools whose validity and significance

are established as people adapt and test them in physical and social settings. For pragmatists, ideas demonstrate their value insofar as they enrich human experience." Microsoft Encarta Online Encyclopedia, "Pragmatism," http://encarta.msn.com/encnet/refpages/search.aspx?q=Pragmatism (accessed September 26, 2008).

255. William James, *The Meaning of Truth* (London: Longmans and Green, 1909), 12-13.

256. Gerald Myers, *William James: His Life and Thought* (New Haven: Yale University Press, 1986), 324.

257. Anton Boisen, *Out of the Depths*, 147.

258. Seward Hiltner, "The Heritage of Anton Boisen," *Pastoral Psychology*, November 1965: 6.

259. Anton Boisen, "The Experiential Aspects of Dementia Praecox," *American Journal of Psychiatry* 13, no. 3 (November 1933). This is a comprehensive report on Boisen's findings regarding the 173 cases at Westboro Hospital and a few at Worcester State Hospital. He writes about the schizophrenic experience using as a reference the case study of Albert W.

260. Boisen, *Exploration of the Inner World*, 28.

261. Charles Hall, Jr.," Some Contributions of Anton Boisen to Understanding Dementia Praecox," *Psychiatry and Religion*, 50-51, box 196, folder 2860, Boisen Collection, Pitts Theological Library, Candler School of Theology, Emory University, Atlanta, Georgia.

262. Boisen, "The Experiential Aspects of Dementia Praecox," 546-548.

263. Boisen, "The Experiential Aspects of Dementia Praecox," 271-273.

264. Richard Cabot, "The Essentials of Case Records for Teaching Purposes," file cabinet 2, drawer 2, in file cabinet 3, bottom drawer, and also in file cabinet 5, top drawer, under "Harvard 1922-

24, " Boisen Collection, Hammond Library, Chicago Theological Seminary, Chicago, Illinois.

265. Anton Boisen, "Religious Experience and Psychological Conflict," *Journal of Pastoral Care* 13, no. 3(1959).

266. Asquith, "The Case Study Method of Anton Boisen," 86.

267. Glenn Asquith, Jr., "The Clinical Method of Theological Inquiry of Anton T. Boisen," (Ph.D. diss., Southern Baptist Theological Seminary, 1976), 156-158, 171-175.

268. Anton Boisen, "Inspiration in the Light of Psychopathology," *Pastoral Psychology*, October 1960.

269. George Coe, "Mysticism," in *Psychology of Religion* (Chicago: The University of Chicago Press, 1916).

270. Boisen, "Inspiration in the Light of Psychopathology."

271. Clarence Bruninga, telephone conversation with the author, September 21, 2006.

272. Anton Boisen, interview by Francis McPeek, 1952, box 235, nos. 1-4, Boisen Collection, Pitts Theology Library Archival Department, Emory University, Atlanta, Georgia.

273. Anton Boisen, "Types of Mental Illness: A Beginning Course for Use in the Training Centers of the Council for Clinical Training of Theological Schools," pt. 1 (1946), Boisen Collection, Hammond Library, Chicago Theological Seminary, Chicago, Illinois.

274. Anton Boisen, *The Exploration of the Inner World*, 160.

275. The pictorials are present in the Boisen Collection, Hammond Library, Chicago Theological Seminary, Chicago, Illinois.

276. Anton T. Boisen, ed., *Hymns of Hope and Courage*, 2nd ed. (Chicago, Illinois, Chicago Theological Seminary, 1950).

277. The ministry of the cure of souls, or pastoral care, consists of helping acts, done by *representative religious people*, directed toward

ENDNOTES

healing, guiding, sustaining, and reconciling with the other.

278. Anton Boisen to Fred Kuether, September 21, 1954, box 195, no. 2356, Anton Boisen Collection, ACPE Archives at Pitts Theological Library, Candler School of Theology, Emory University, Atlanta, Georgia.

279. Homer Ashby, *Reclaiming the Soul of the Cure of Souls* (lecture at McCormick Seminary, 1996), quoted in Herbert Anderson, "Whatever Happened *to Seelsorge?*" *Word and World* (Seattle, Washington: Seattle University School of Theology and Ministry).

280. Herbert Anderson, "Whatever Happened *to Seelsorge?*" *Word and World* (Seattle, Washington: Seattle University School of Theology and Ministry).

281. "A Page of the Blessed Virgin" (case history of a 20-year-old Roman Catholic housekeeper, nurse's aide, and cook who was a patient at Elgin State Hospital), file cabinet 1, drawer 1, Boisen Collection, Hammond Library, Chicago Theological Seminary, Chicago, Illinois.

282. Anton T. Boisen, "Problems in Religion and Life for Pastors," (typed mimeographed document, 1946), box 196, file 2859, Anton Boisen Collection, Pitts Theological Library , Candler School of Theology, Emory University, Atlanta, Georgia.

283. Arthur Cushman McGiffert, "Memories of Anton T. Boisen," videotaped interview, July 26, 1986.

284. Anton Boisen, "Our Objectives" (lecture, Conference for the Council for the Clinical Training of Theological Students at Worcester State Hospital, August 23, 1930), mimeographed copy from the author's file, 1 and 2.

285. Boisen, "Our Objectives," 2.

286. Boisen, "Problems of Religion and Life."

287. Anton Boisen, "The Challenge to Our Seminaries," *Christian Work*, January 23, 1926: 11.

288. Asquith, "The Clinical Method of Theological Inquiry of Anton T. Boisen," 118.

289. Asquith, "The Clinical Method of Theological Inquiry of Anton T. Boisen," 117.

290. Boisen, *Exploration of the Inner World*, 306.

291. Anton Boisen, "Cooperative Inquiry in Religion," *Religious Education*, October 1945: 293, box 197, file No. 2859, Anton Boisen Collection, Pitts Theology Library, Emory University, Atlanta, Georgia.

292. Boisen, *Exploration of the Inner World*, 191.

293. John L. Cedarleaf, "Anton Boisen—A Memoir," *Cura Animarum*, (Decatur, GA: Association of Mental Health Clergy, Journal o f Pastoral Care Publications, Inc., 1992), 59-65.

294. Henri J. M. Nouwen, "Boisen and Coe," mimeographed copy, John M. Kelly Library Archives and Research Collection, University of St. Michael's College, Toronto, Ontario, Canada.

295. Cedarleaf, "Anton Boisen—A Memoir," 59.

296. Boisen, *Exploration of the Inner World*, ch. 7,181- 215.

297. Boisen, *Religion in Crisis and Custom* (New York: Harper and Brothers, 1945), 19.

298. Boisen, *Religion in Crisis and Custom*, 3.

299. Hall, *Head and Heart*, 12.

300. Boisen, *Exploration of the Inner World*, 299. On the "idea of God" see also Asquith, "The Clinical Method of Theological Inquiry of Anton T. Boisen, "122-123.

301. Leo Tolstoy, *The Death of Ivan Ilych and Other Stories*, trans. Rosemary Edmonds (Middlesex, England: Penguin Classics Ltd., 1960).

302. Glenn Asquith, "An Experiential Theology," *Turning Points in Pastoral Care*, 24.

303. John Patton, " Dicks-Boisen Lecture" (paper given at The Association of Professional Chaplains, Atlanta, GA, May 10, 2006).

304. Stanley Hauerwas, *The Peaceable Kingdom* (South Bend, Indiana: University of Notre Dame Press, 2002), 24.

305. Asquith, *The Clinical Method of Theological Inquiry of Anton. T. Boisen,* 147.

306. The Covenanters were Scottish Presbyterians of the 17th century who subscribed to covenants, including the *National Covenant* of 1638, the most famous being the *Solemn League and Covenant of 1643.* The National Covenant opposed the new Anglican liturgy introduced in1637 by King Charles I. This led to the abolition of episcopacy in Scotland and the Bishops' Wars (1639-41), in which the Scots successfully defended their religious freedom against Charles I. In the *Solemn League and Covenant,* the Scots pledged their support to the English parliamentarians in the English Civil War with the hope that Presbyterianism would become the established church in England. They did not succeed in this effort, although Presbyterianism did become the official religion of Scotland.

307. Boisen, *Theme for Our Objectives* (speech, Worcester State Hospital, Council for Clinical Training of Theological Students Conference, 1935), 1, Archives of Journal of Clinical Pastoral Education, Inc., Pitts Theological Library, Emory University, Atlanta, Georgia.

308. Thornton, "Some Hard Questions for Clinical Pastoral Education," *Journal of Pastoral Care* 22, no. 4 (December 1968): 197-198.

309 Thomas O'Conner, *Clinical Pastoral Supervision and the Theology of Charles Gerkin* (Canadian Corporation for Studies in Religion, Wilfrid Laurier University Press, 1998), 43.

310. Boisen, *The Exploration of the Inner World,* 185.

311. McGiffert, interviewed by Earl Cooper, J. Lennart Cedarleaf and Herman Eichorn, Claremont School of Theology, July 24, 1986.

312. Arthur Cushman McGiffert, "Doctor of Letters, *honoris causa*," Boisen Collection, Hammond Library, Chicago Theological Seminary, Chicago, Illinois.

313. Frederic Norstad, "Science in Christian Perspective," *Journal of American Scientific Affiliation* 14 (December 1962): 99-103.

314. Clarence Bruninga, telephone conversation with the author on May 3, 2006.

315. Henri J. M. Nouwen, "Boisen," mimeographed paper on an interview with Anton Boisen, August 1964, Henri J. M Nouwen Archives at the University of St Michael's College, University of Toronto, Toronto, Ontario, Canada.

316. Nouwen, "Boisen."

317. James Gibbons, e-mail message to the author, August 20, 2007.

318. Thomas Klink, "Anton T. Boisen: A Remembrance of the Committal of His Ashes," *The Journal of Pastoral Care* 19, no. 4 (Winter 1965): 230, as quoted in *A Vision from a Little Known Country*, Glenn Asquith, Jr., ed. (Journal of Pastoral Care Publications, 1992), 12

LaVergne, TN USA
10 December 2009
56548LV00002B/19/P